# Un-Color-It Activity Books for Adults & Teens

## Hidden Gardens 2 - The Coloring Book That's In Reverse

This activity book has the colors - You draw the lines - Use your imagination to complete the hidden artwork

Kat Mariaca

MadaketLanePublishers@comcast.net

Mariaca, Kat
**Un-Color-It™ Activity Books for Adults & Teens - Hidden Gardens 2: The Adult Coloring Book That's In Reverse**

ISBN: 978-1-940892-39-9

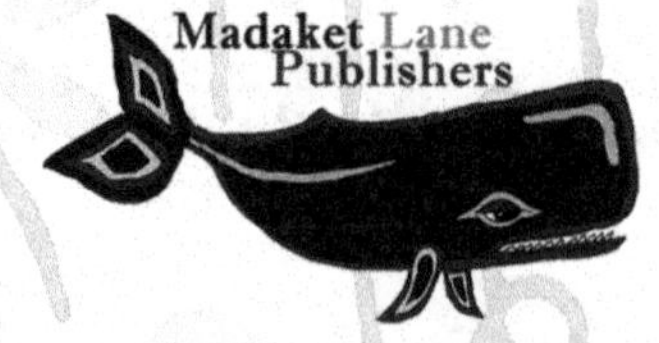

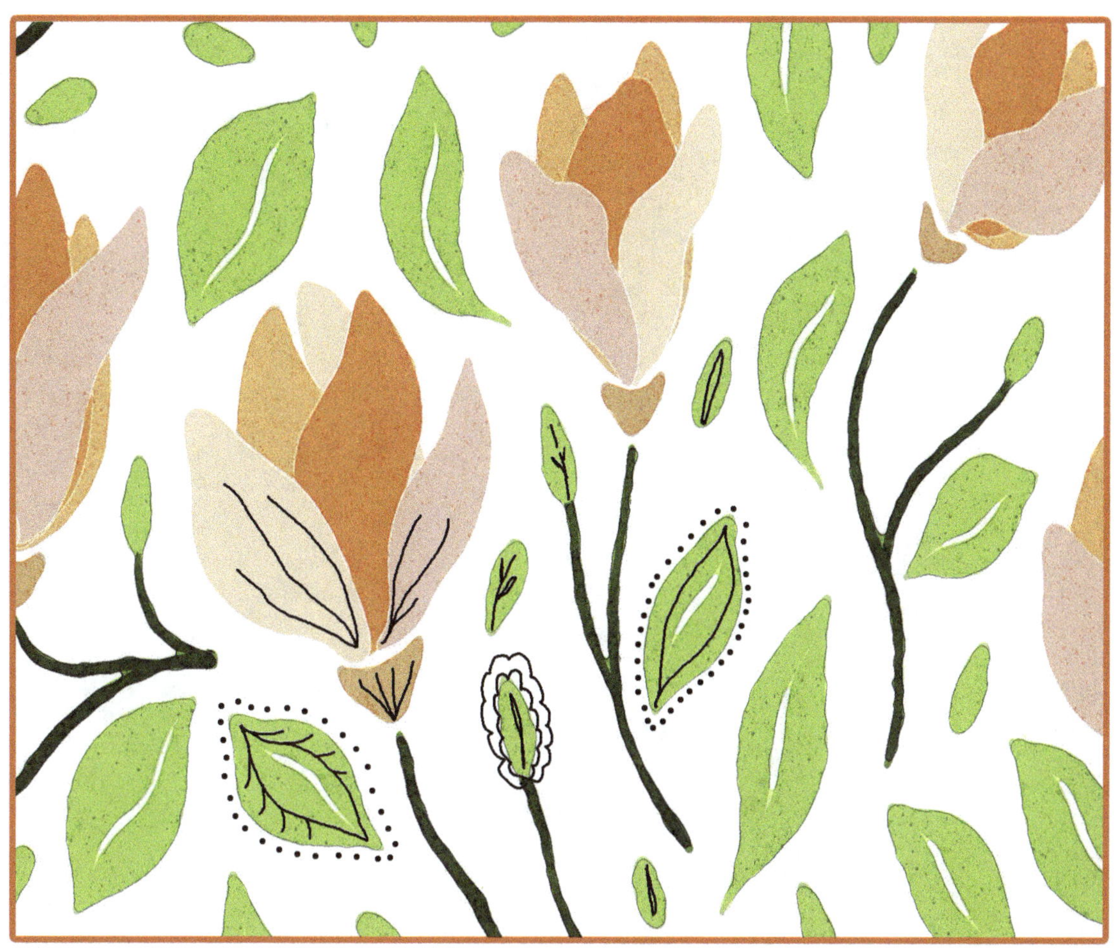

## UN-COLOR-IT!

Uncover the secrets of these beautiful watercolor gardens as you let your imagination flow. Add frames, lines, flourishes, patterns, doodles, swirls, tangles, shades and shadows...anything that excites your eye and delights your creativity. Use pens, pencils, crayons, whatever you enjoy.

I've designed this activity book with each design centered and framed on a page so that you can cut the pages out for framing, or to make coloring more comfortable. Color in the white spaces, or draw over the colored spaces. Keep the pages inside the book, or cut them out to draw on a flat surface.

Happy un-coloring!

*Kat*

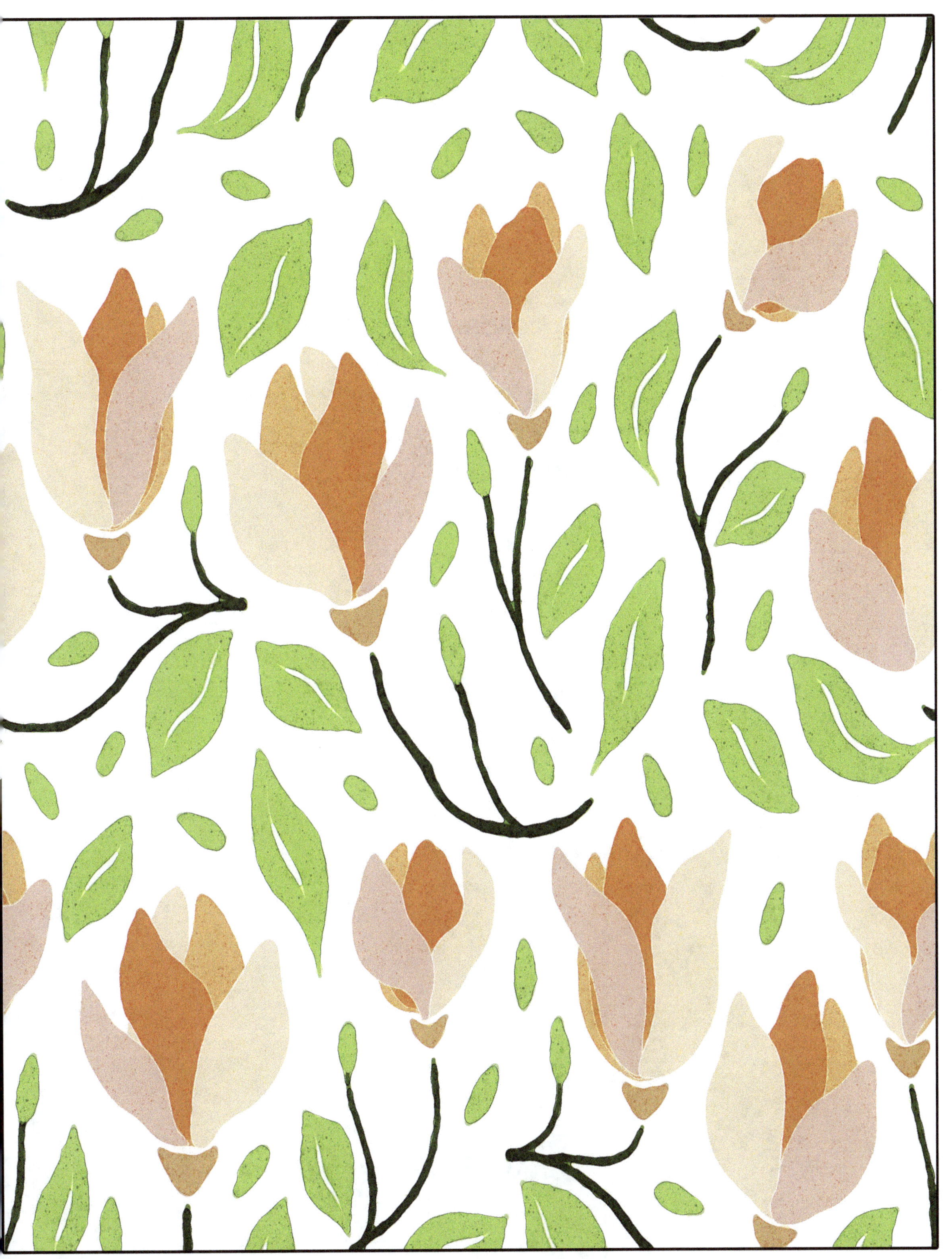

This page deliberately left blank.

As some markers can bleed through,
you may want to place a piece of paper, or wax paper,
between images.

This page deliberately left blank.

As some markers can bleed through,
you may want to place a piece of paper, or wax paper,
between images.

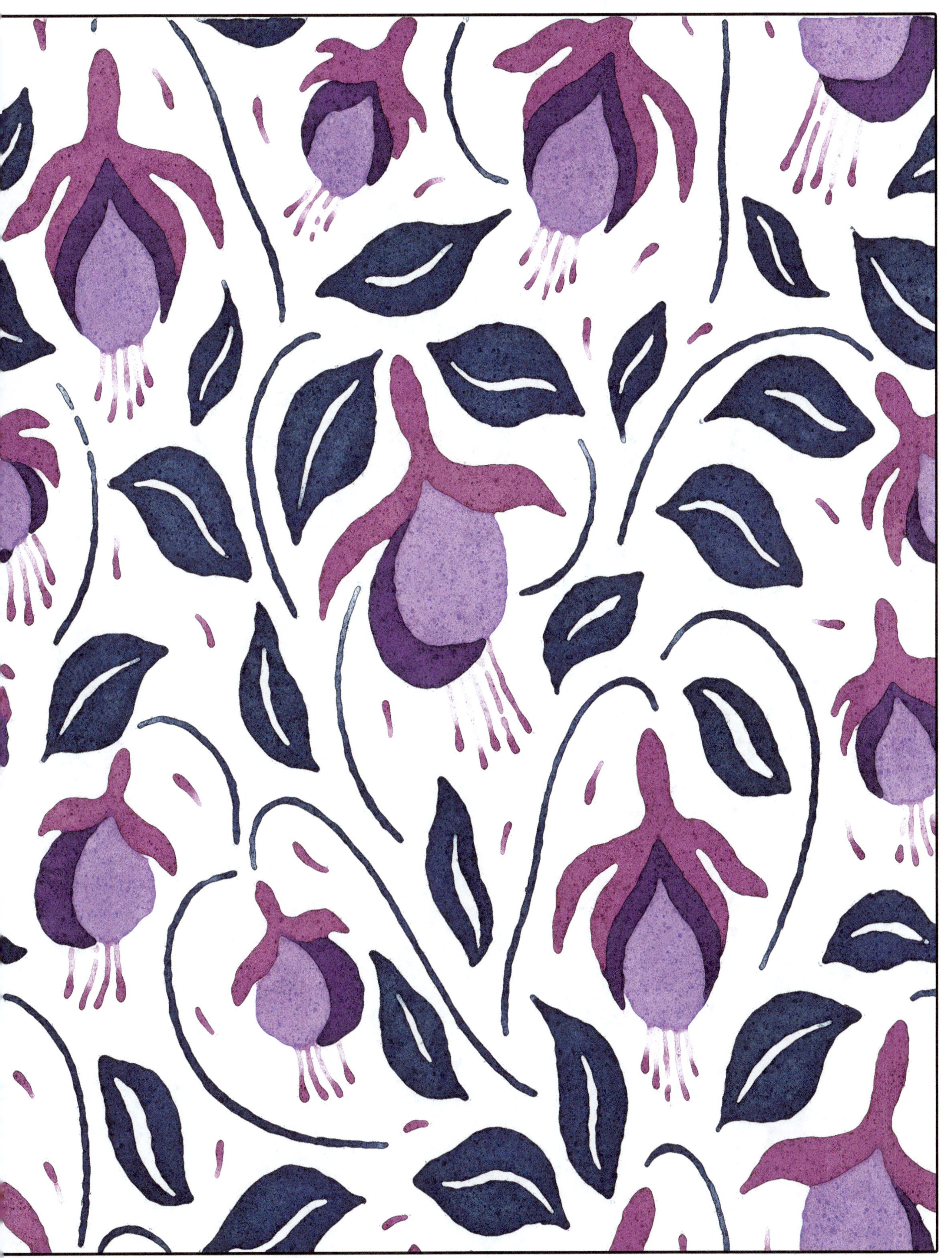

This page deliberately left blank.

As some markers can bleed through,
you may want to place a piece of paper, or wax paper,
between images.

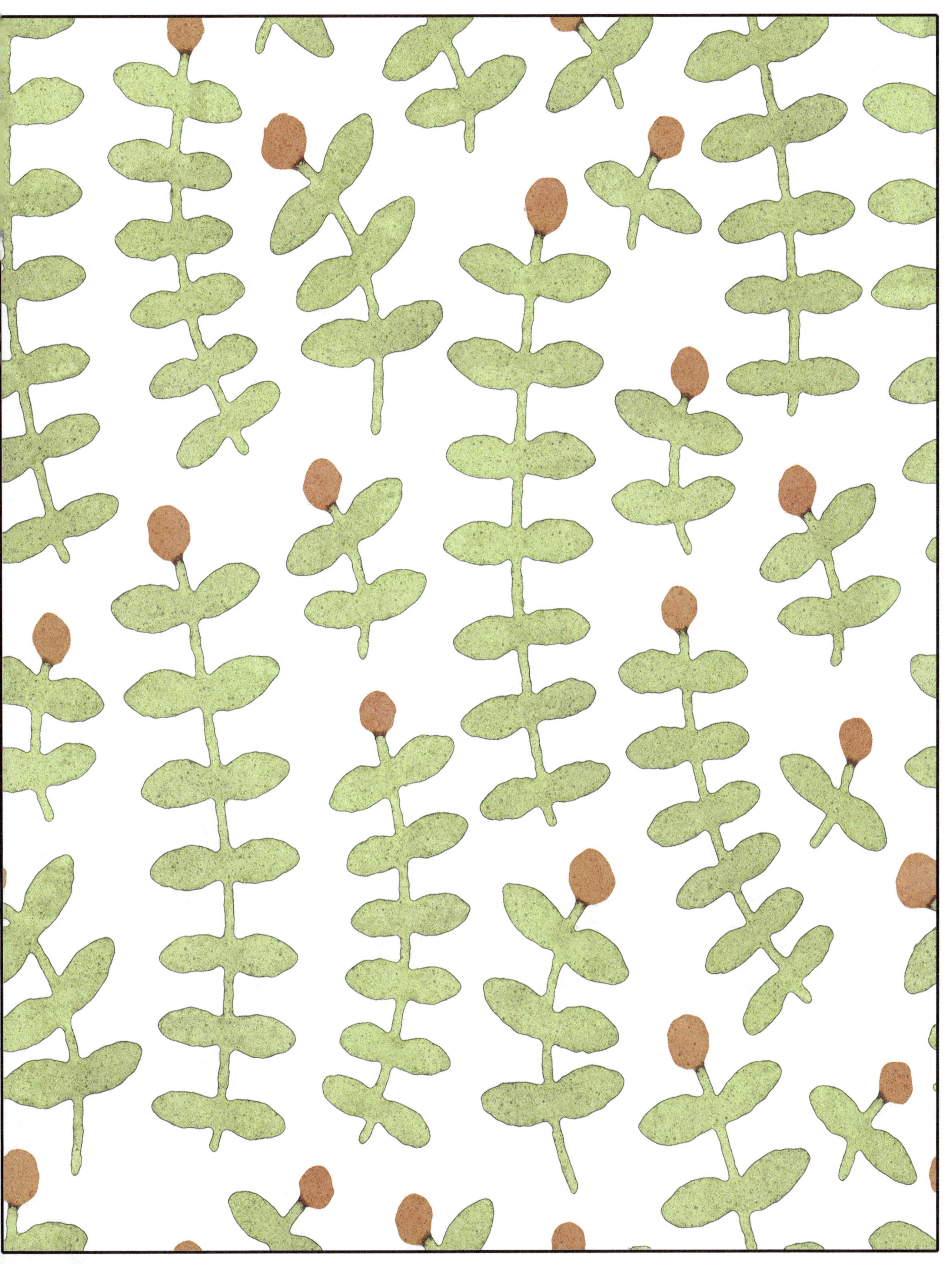

This page deliberately left blank.

As some markers can bleed through,
you may want to place a piece of paper, or wax paper,
between images.

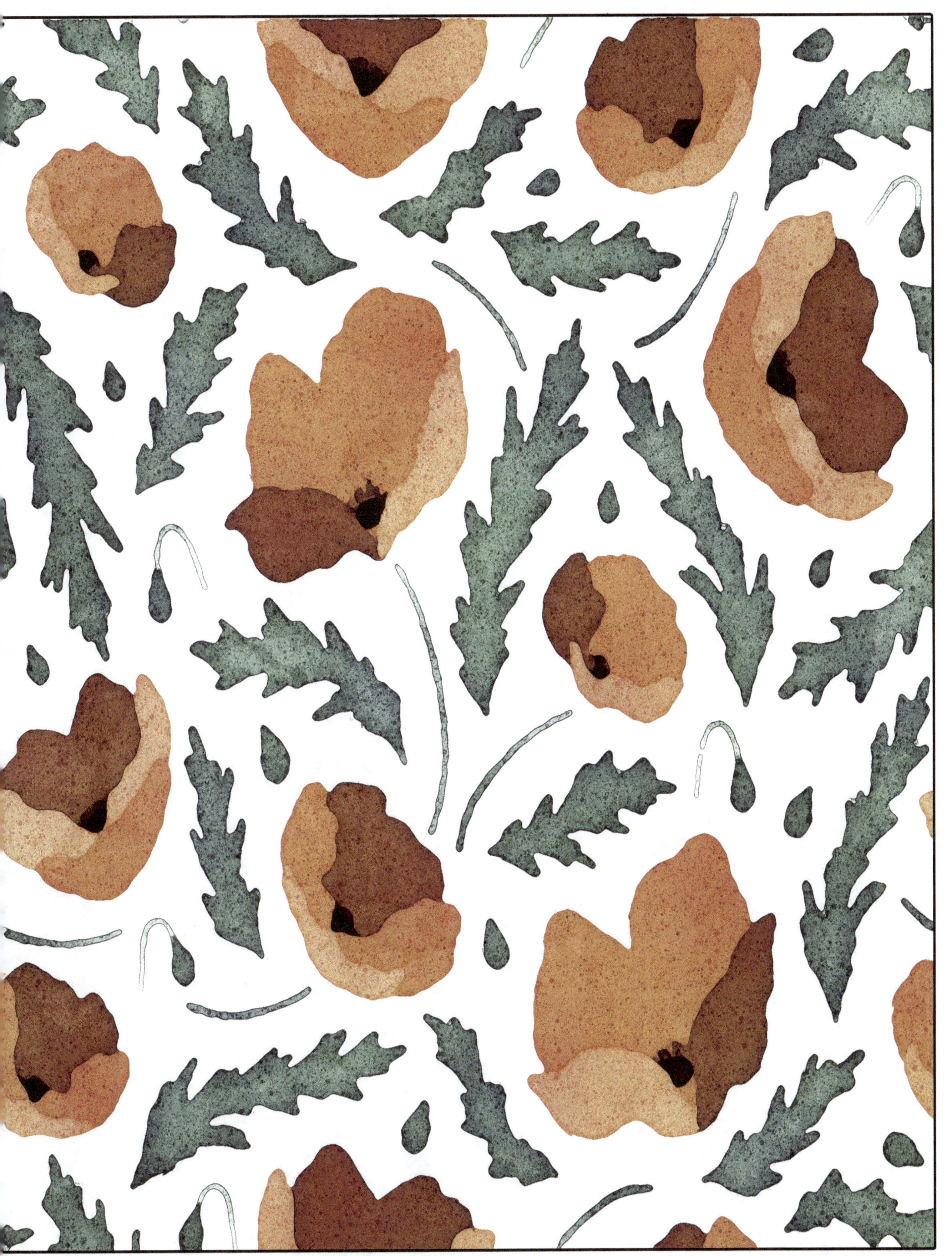

This page deliberately left blank.

As some markers can bleed through,
you may want to place a piece of paper, or wax paper,
between images.

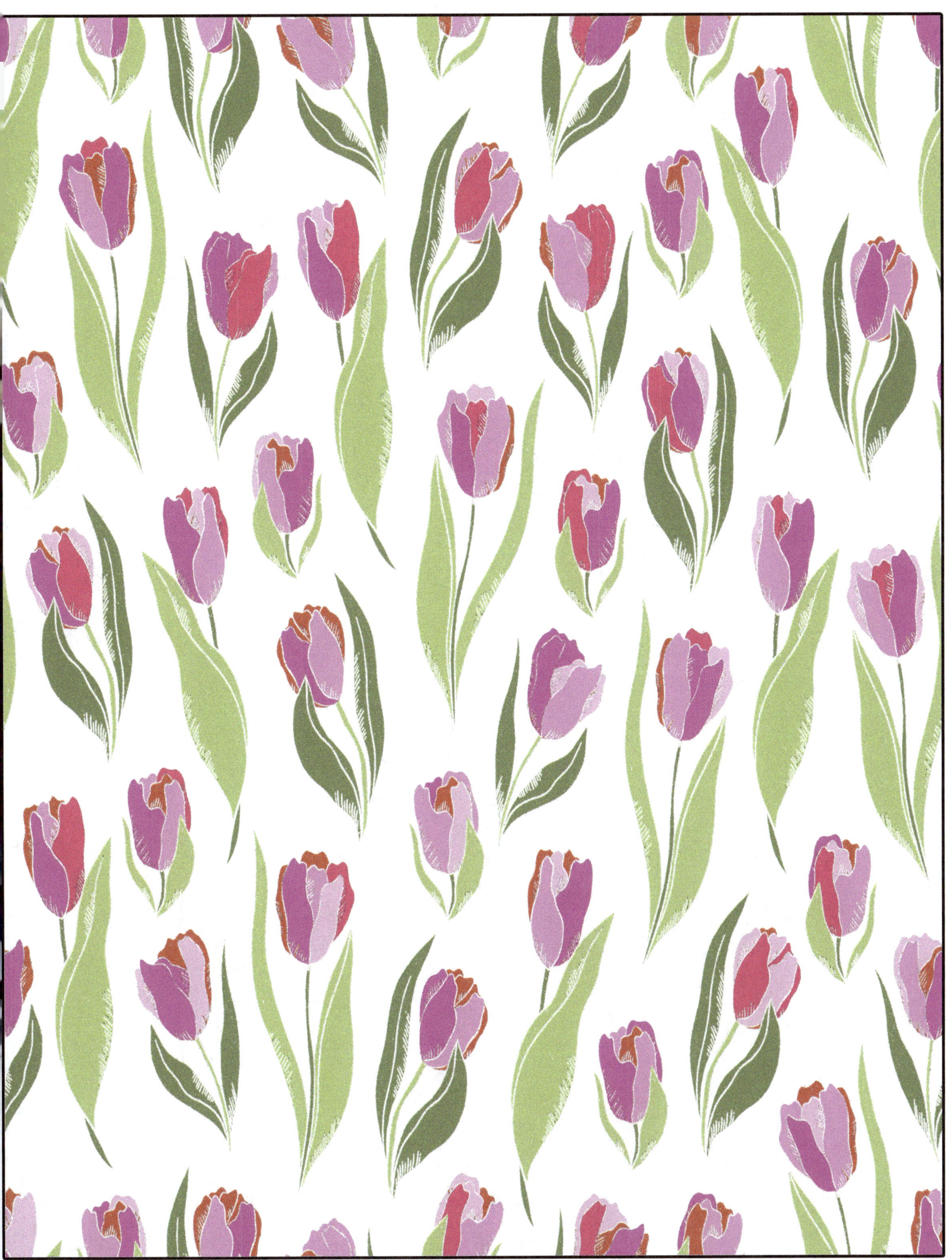

This page deliberately left blank.

As some markers can bleed through,
you may want to place a piece of paper, or wax paper,
between images.

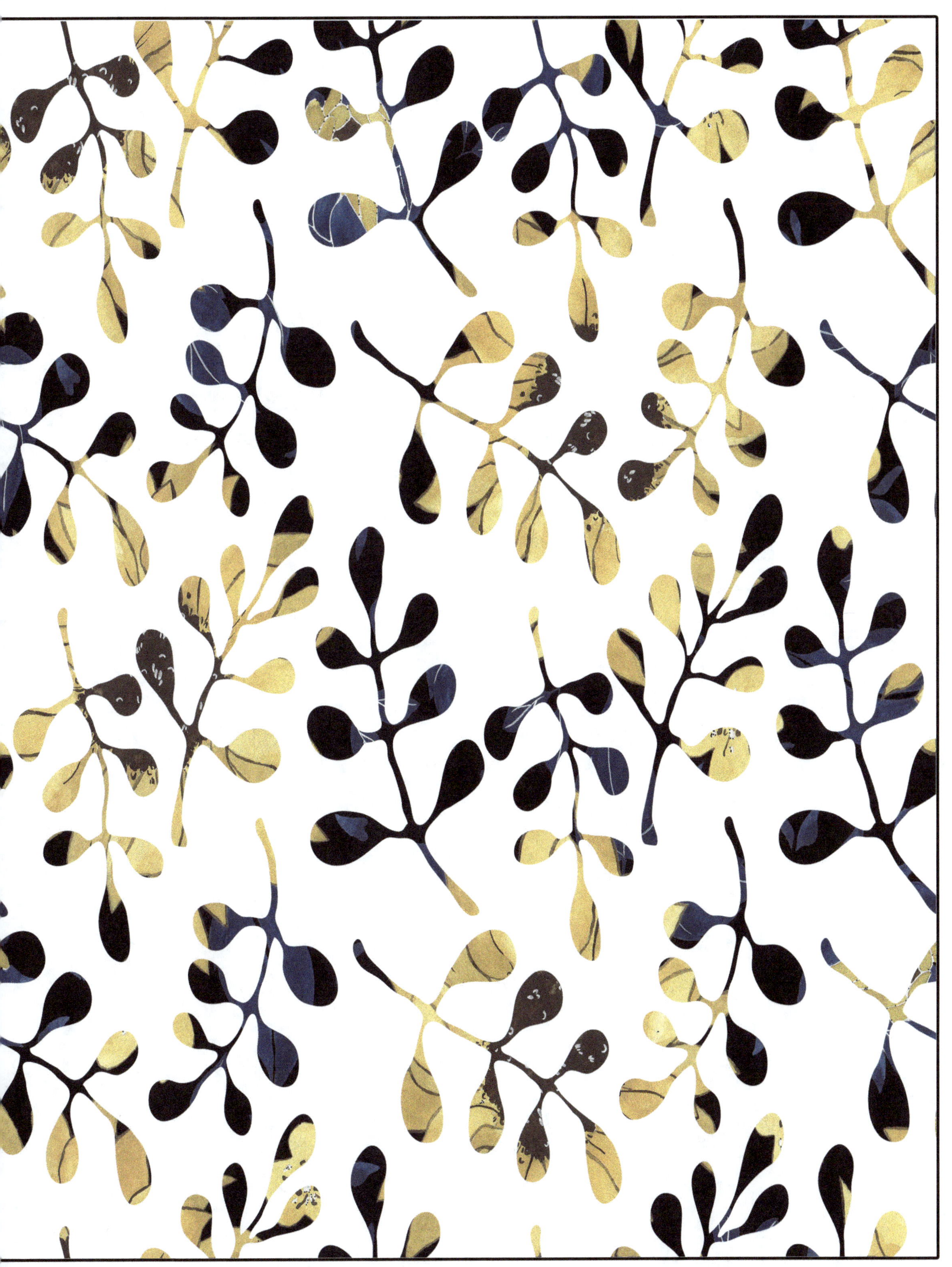

This page deliberately left blank.

As some markers can bleed through,
you may want to place a piece of paper, or wax paper,
between images.

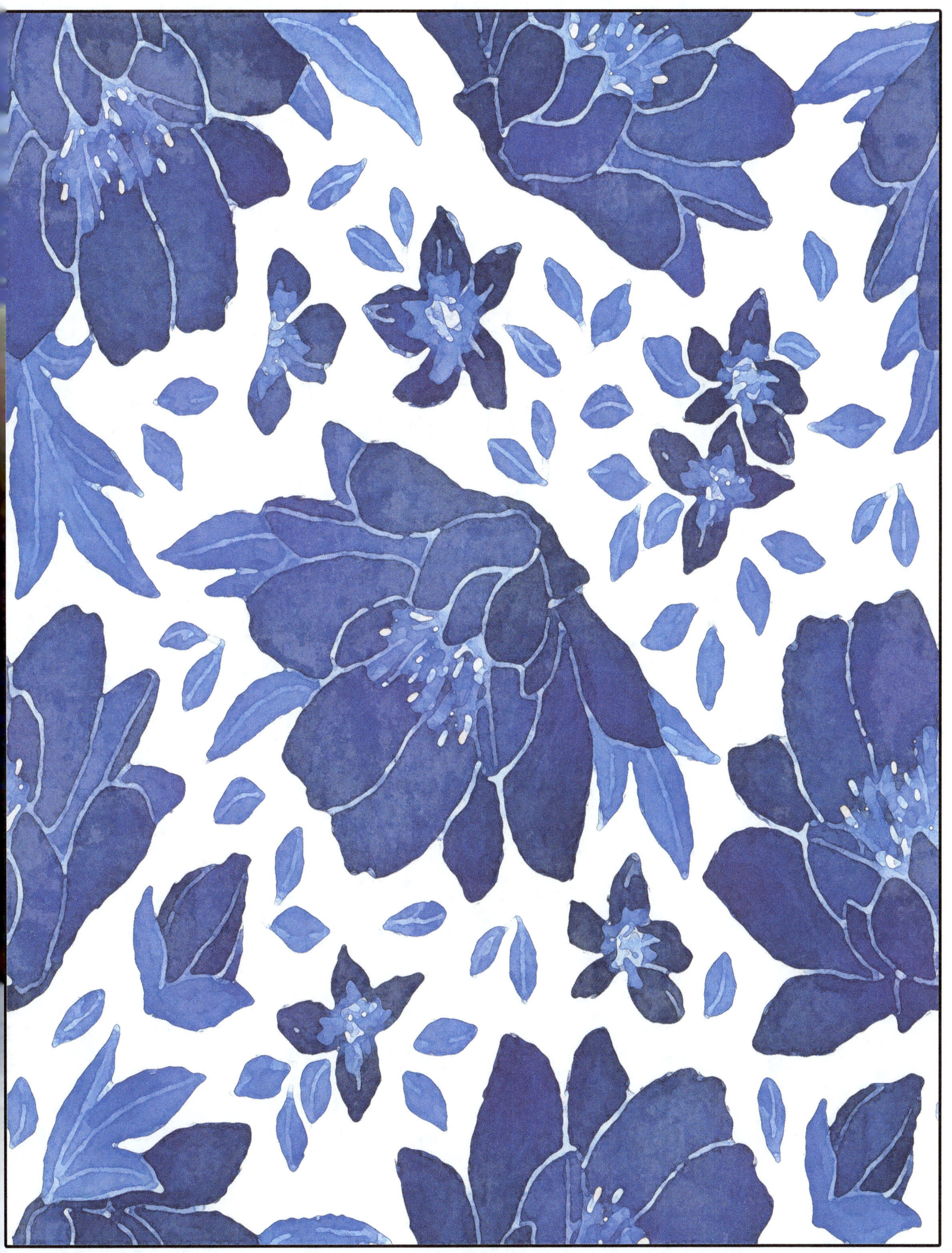

This page deliberately left blank.

As some markers can bleed through,
you may want to place a piece of paper, or wax paper,
between images.

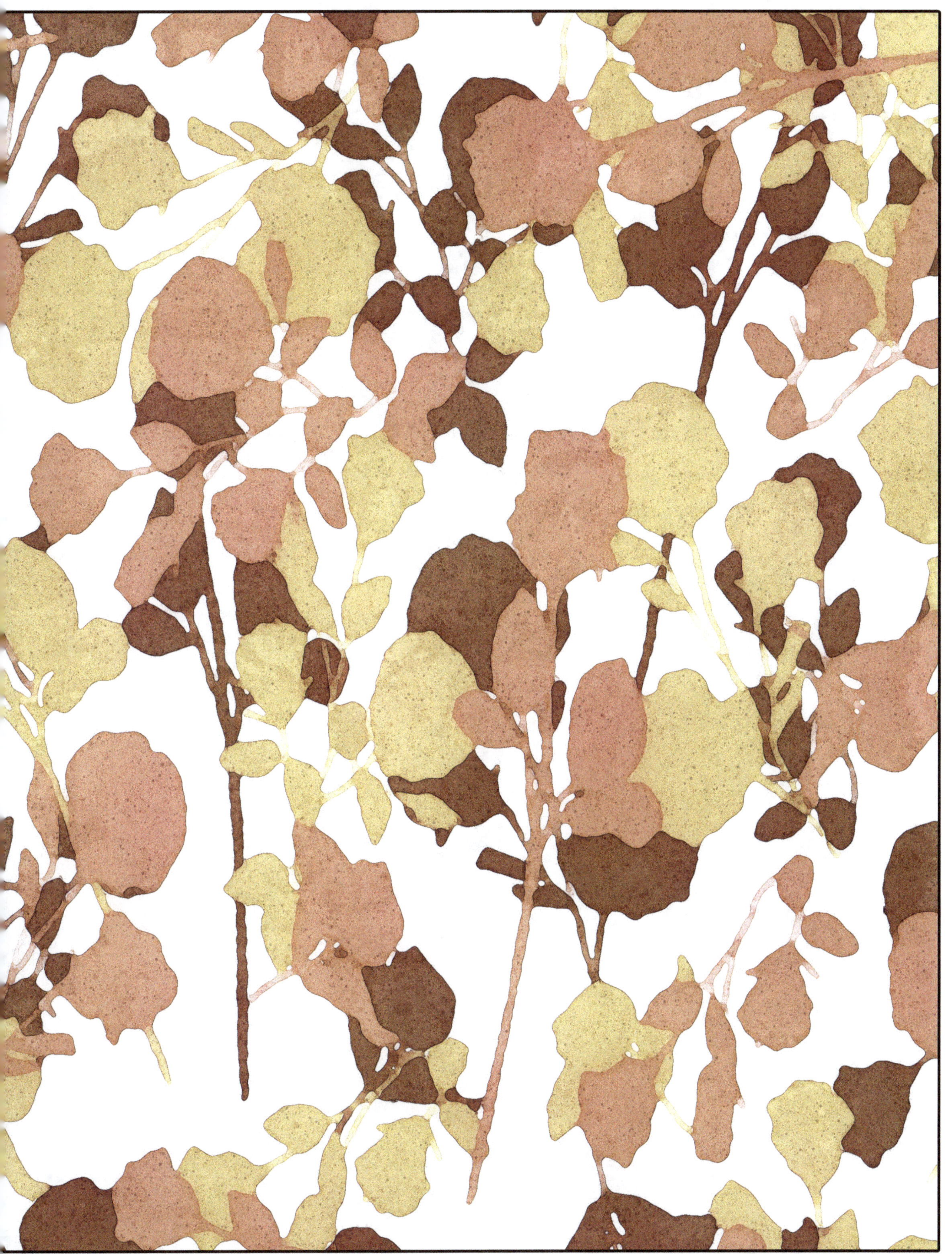

This page deliberately left blank.

As some markers can bleed through,
you may want to place a piece of paper, or wax paper,
between images.

www.Etsy.com/shop/AdornCreatives

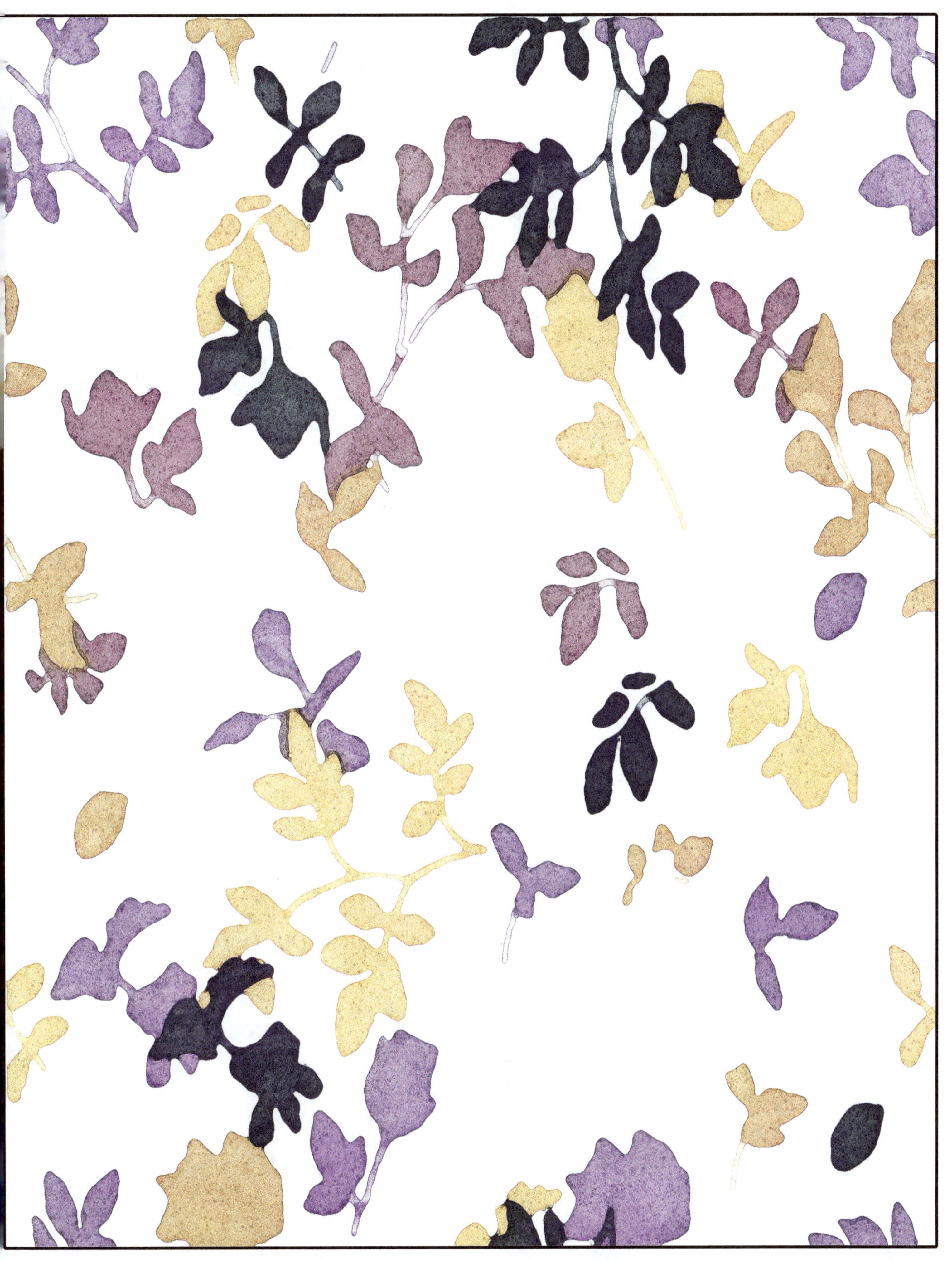

This page deliberately left blank.

As some markers can bleed through,
you may want to place a piece of paper, or wax paper,
between images.

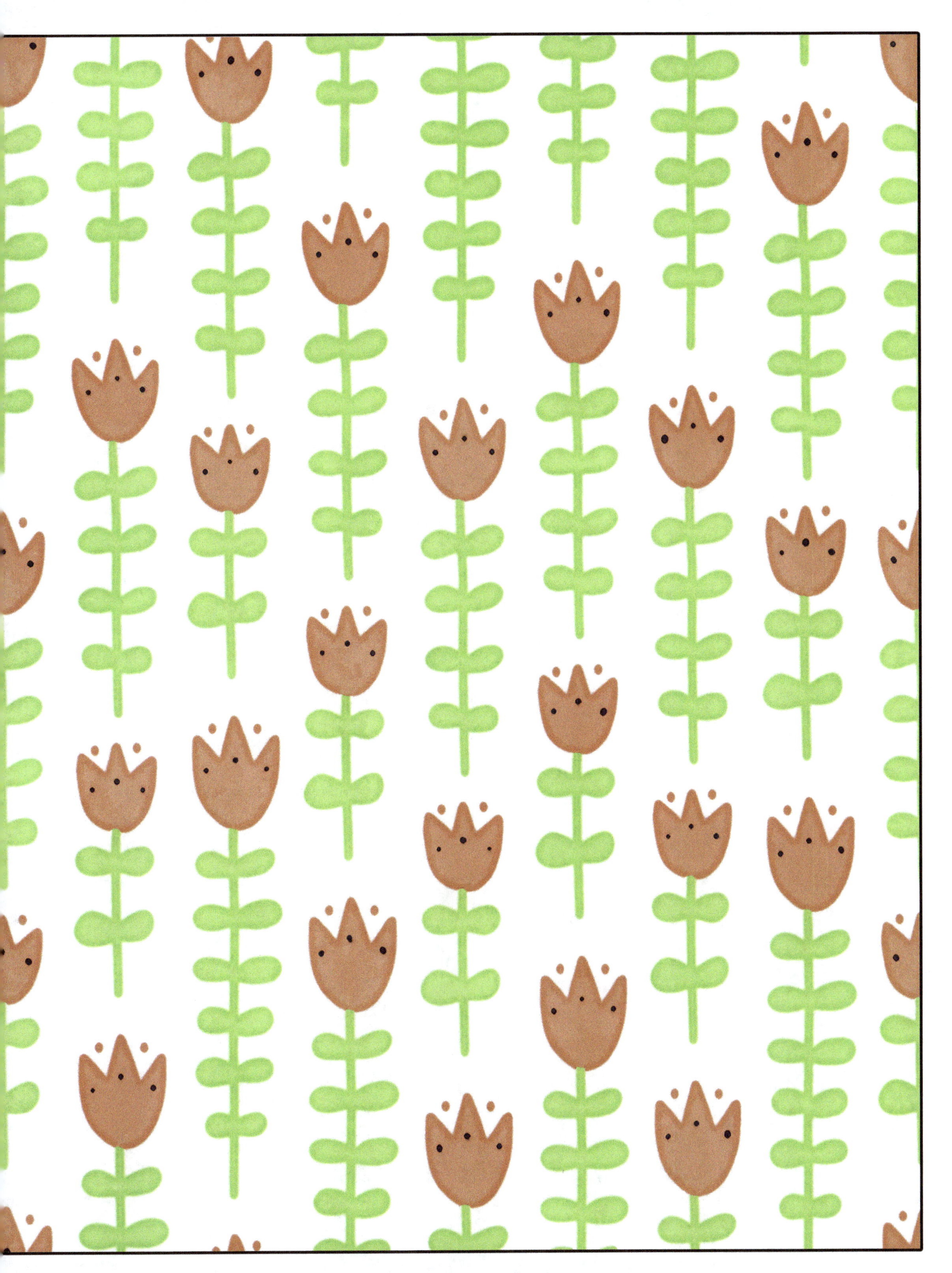

This page deliberately left blank.

As some markers can bleed through,
you may want to place a piece of paper, or wax paper,
between images.

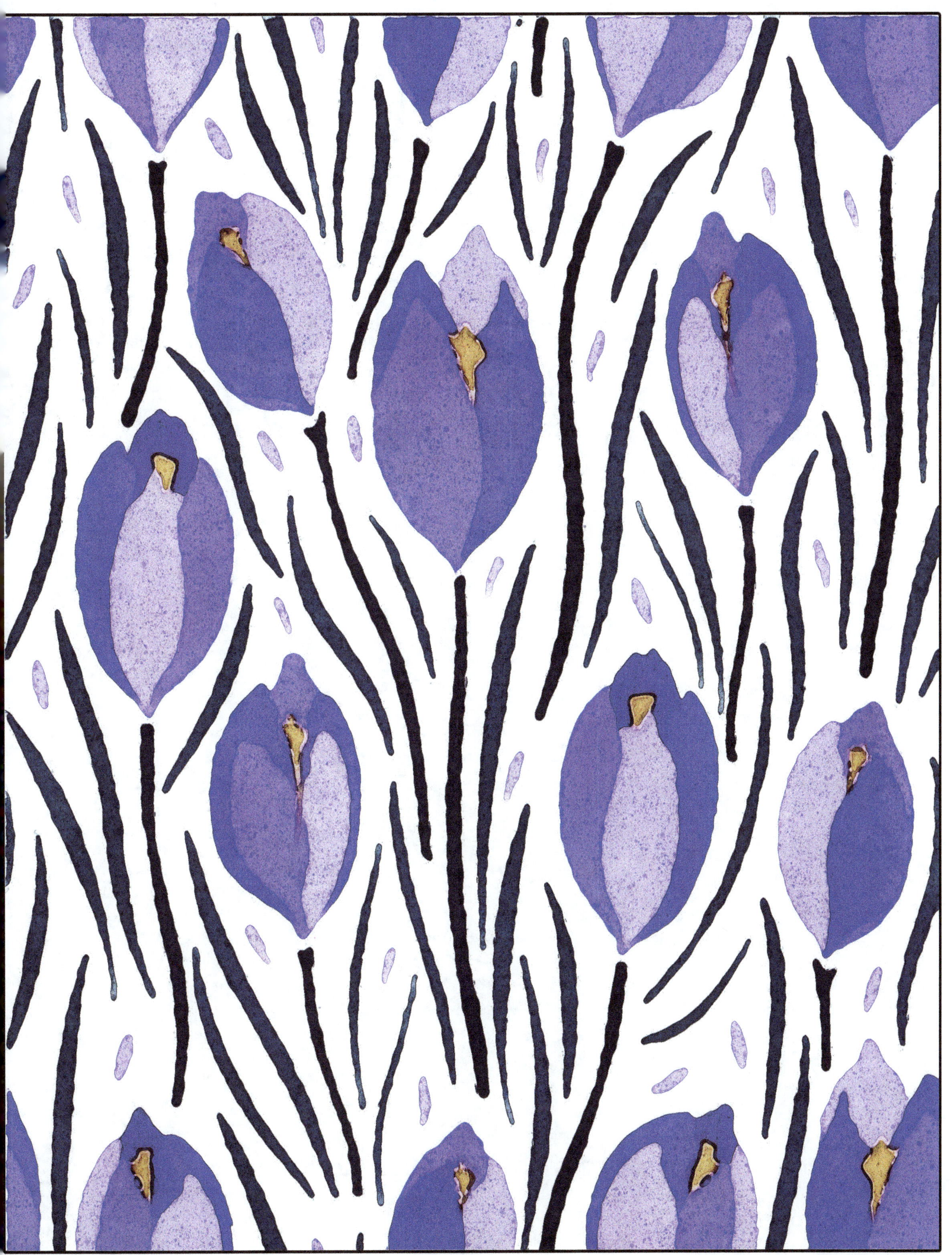

This page deliberately left blank.

As some markers can bleed through,
you may want to place a piece of paper, or wax paper,
between images.

This page deliberately left blank.

As some markers can bleed through,
you may want to place a piece of paper, or wax paper,
between images.

This page deliberately left blank.

As some markers can bleed through,
you may want to place a piece of paper, or wax paper,
between images.

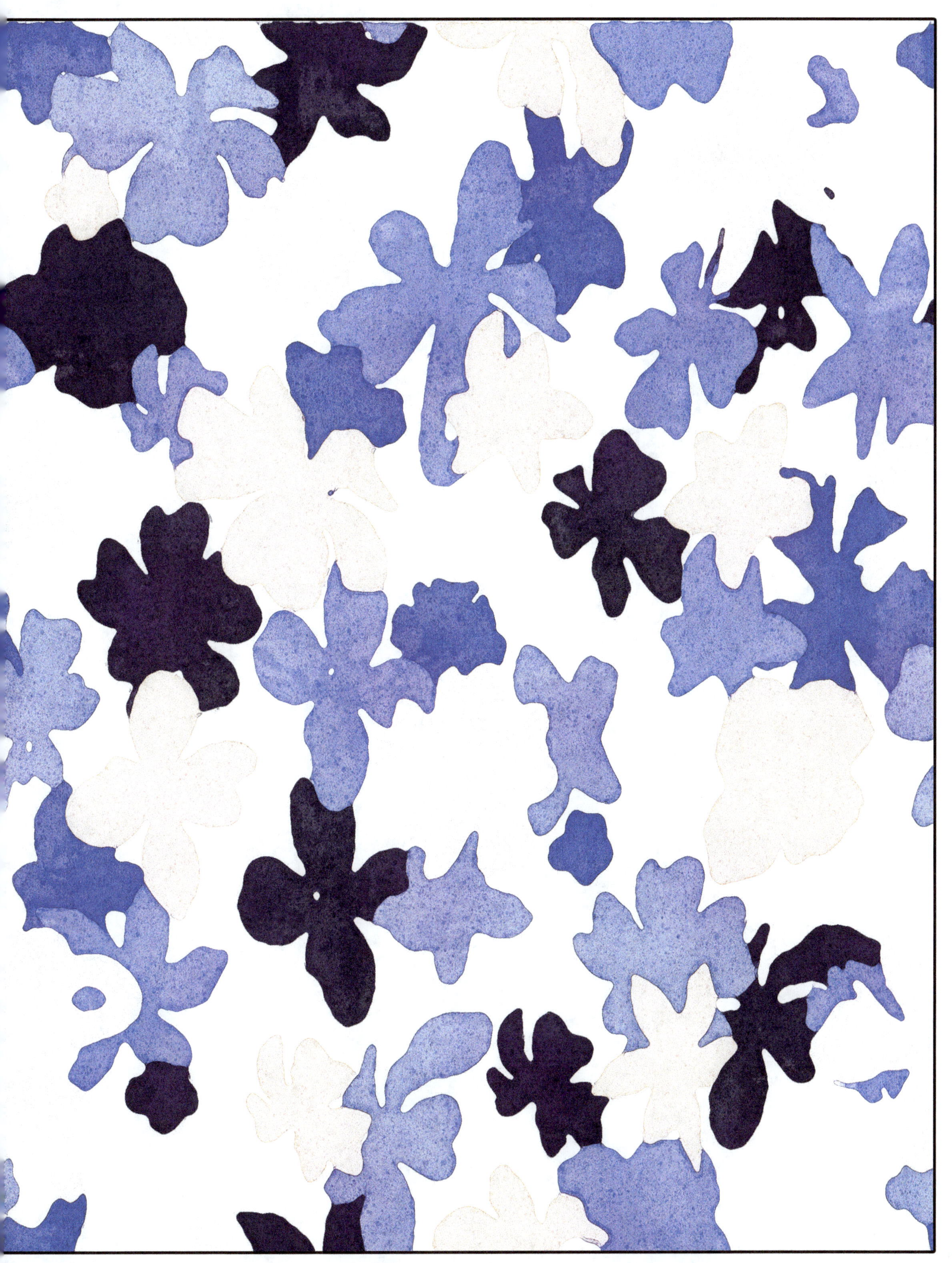

This page deliberately left blank.

As some markers can bleed through,
you may want to place a piece of paper, or wax paper,
between images.

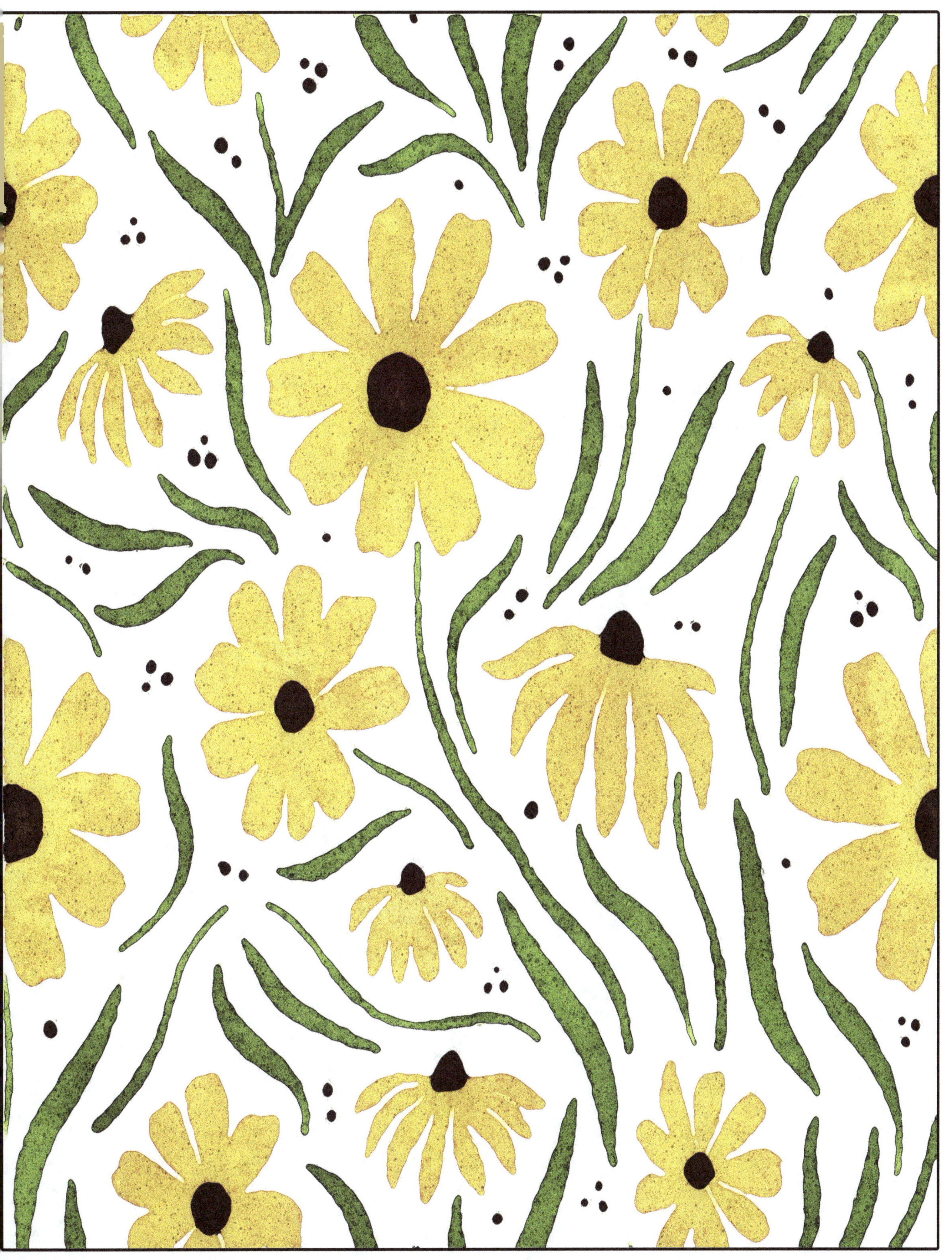

This page deliberately left blank.

As some markers can bleed through,
you may want to place a piece of paper, or wax paper,
between images.

This page deliberately left blank.

As some markers can bleed through,
you may want to place a piece of paper, or wax paper,
between images.

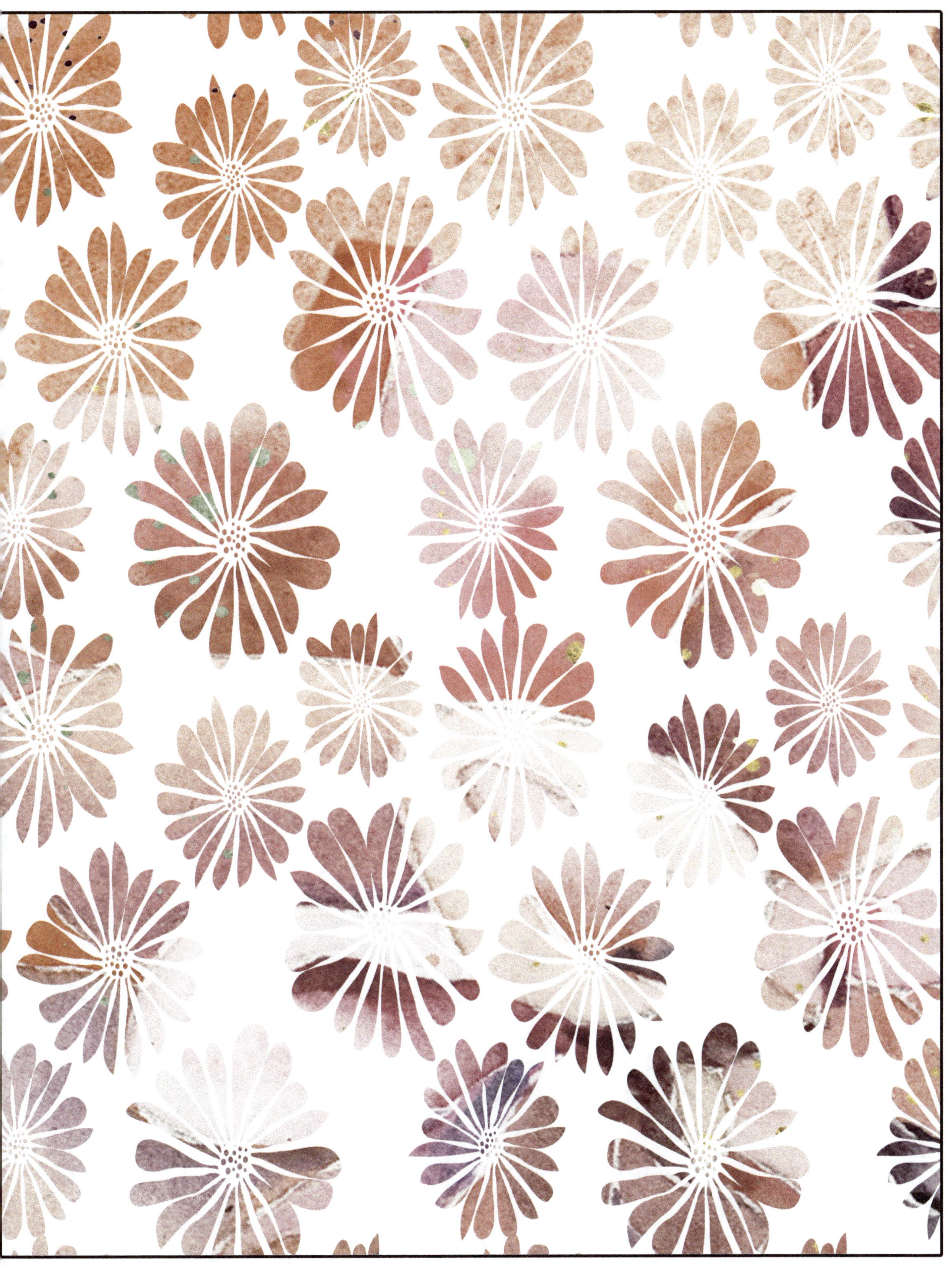

This page deliberately left blank.

As some markers can bleed through,
you may want to place a piece of paper, or wax paper,
between images.

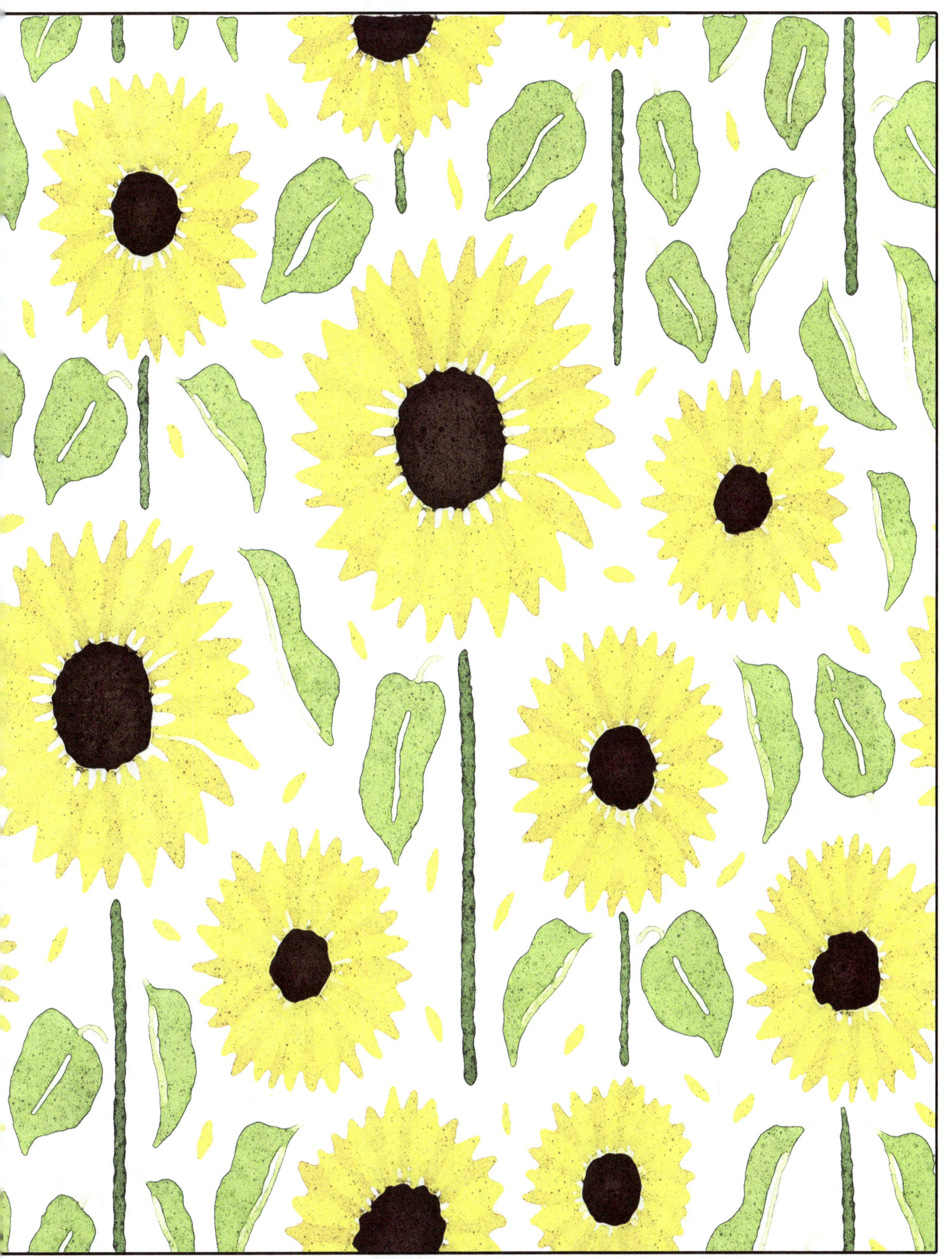

This page deliberately left blank.

As some markers can bleed through,
you may want to place a piece of paper, or wax paper,
between images.

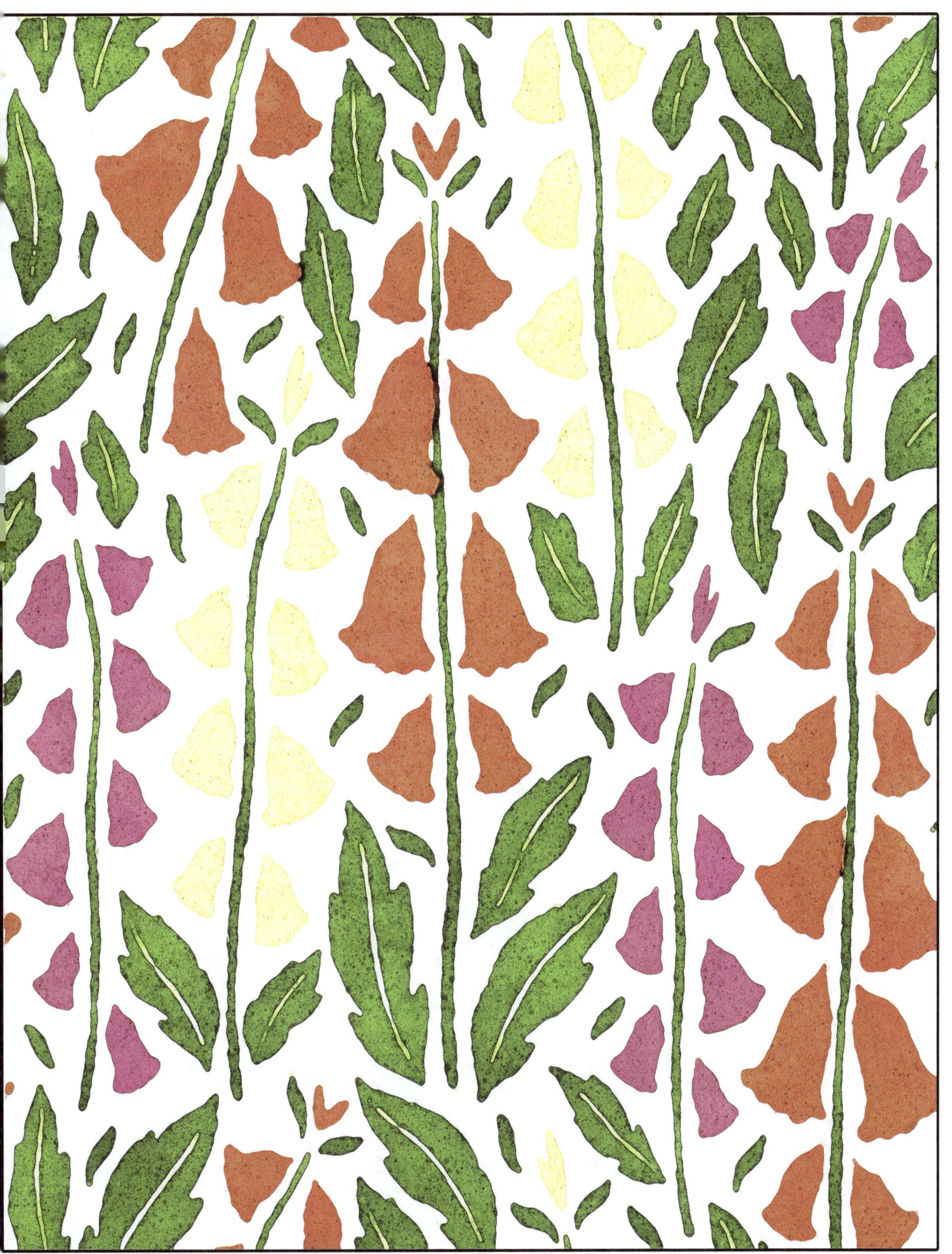

This page deliberately left blank.

As some markers can bleed through,
you may want to place a piece of paper, or wax paper,
between images.

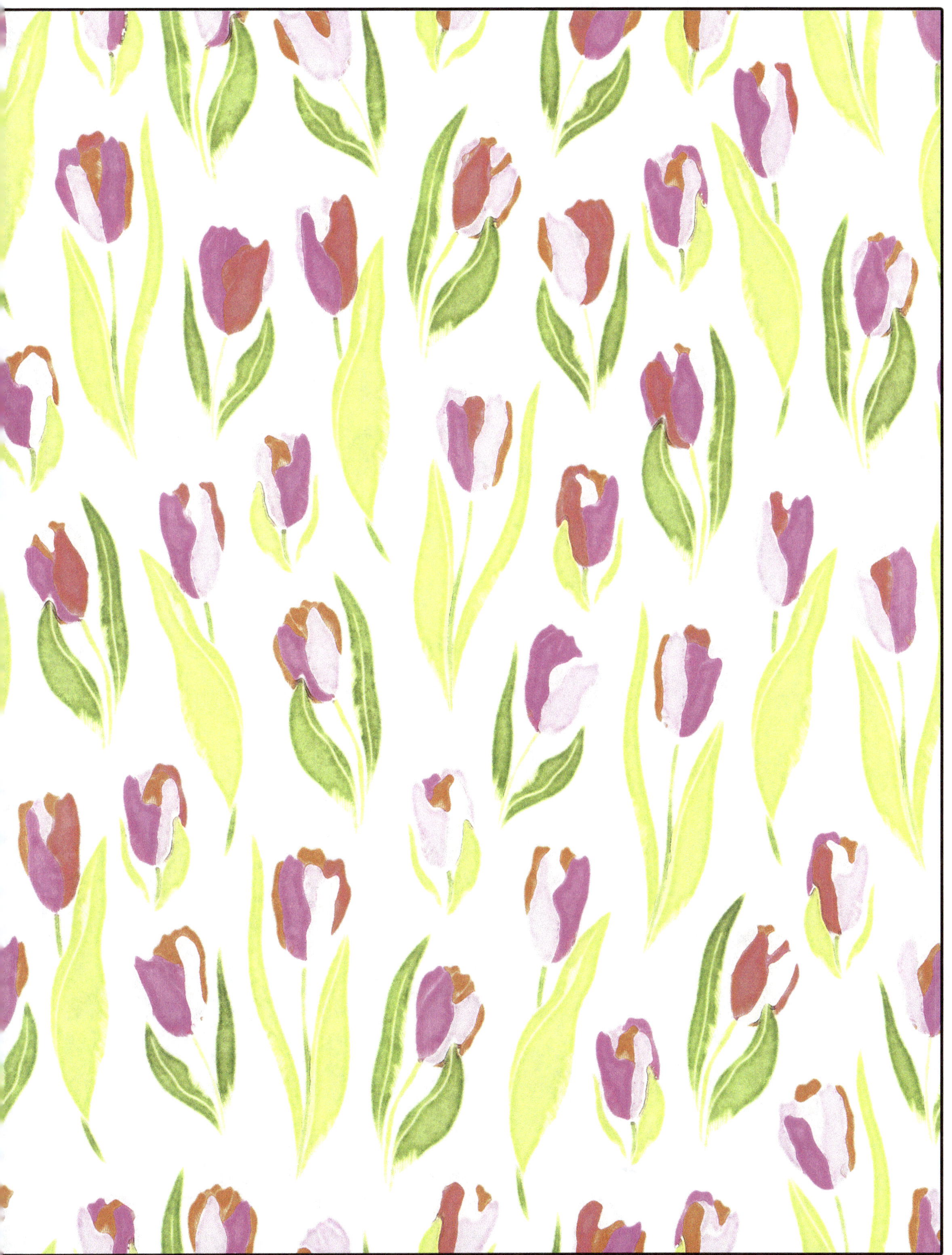

This page deliberately left blank.

As some markers can bleed through,
you may want to place a piece of paper, or wax paper,
between images.

This page deliberately left blank.

As some markers can bleed through,
you may want to place a piece of paper, or wax paper,
between images.

This page deliberately left blank.

As some markers can bleed through,
you may want to place a piece of paper, or wax paper,
between images.

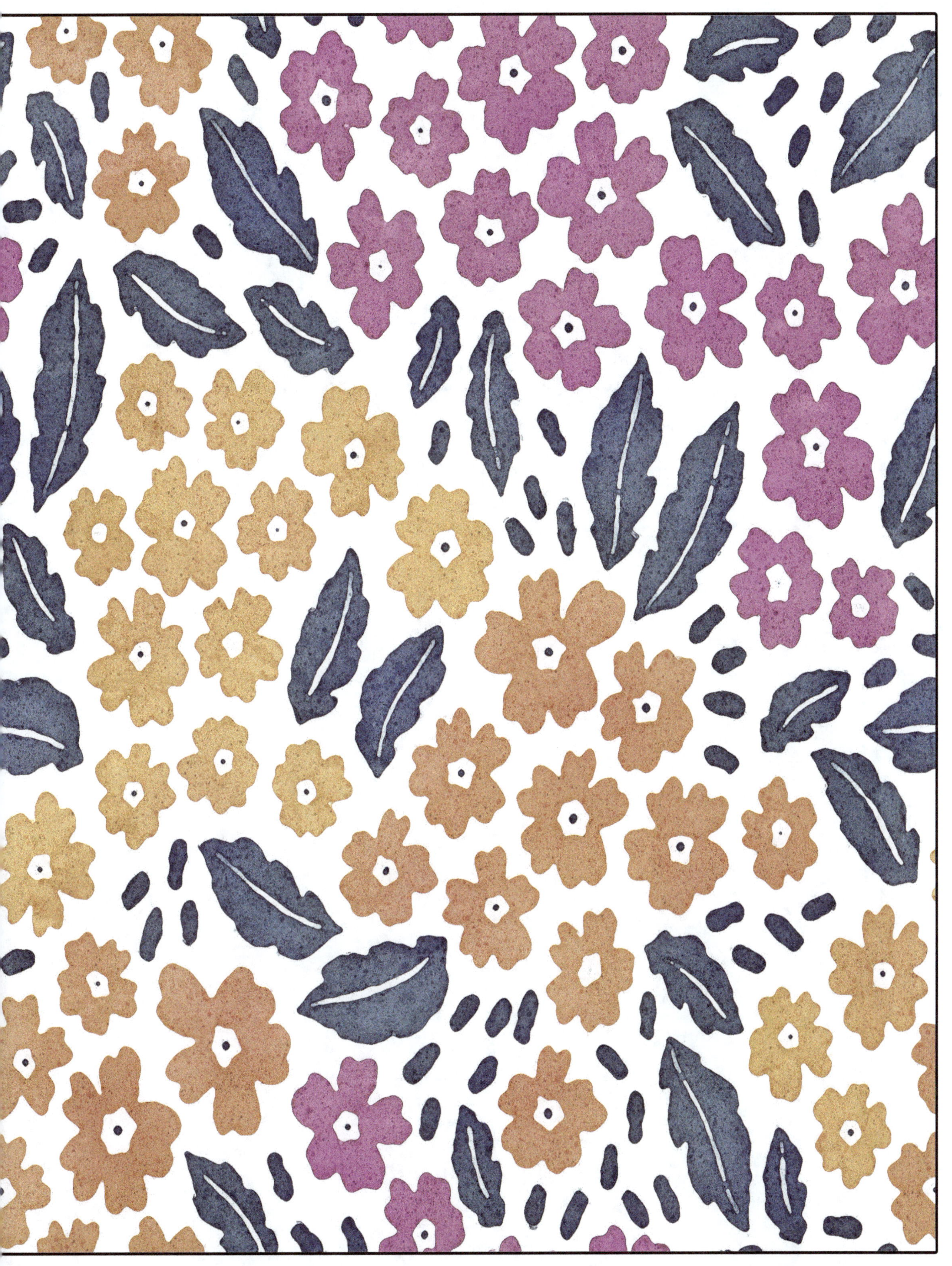

This page deliberately left blank.

As some markers can bleed through,
you may want to place a piece of paper, or wax paper,
between images.

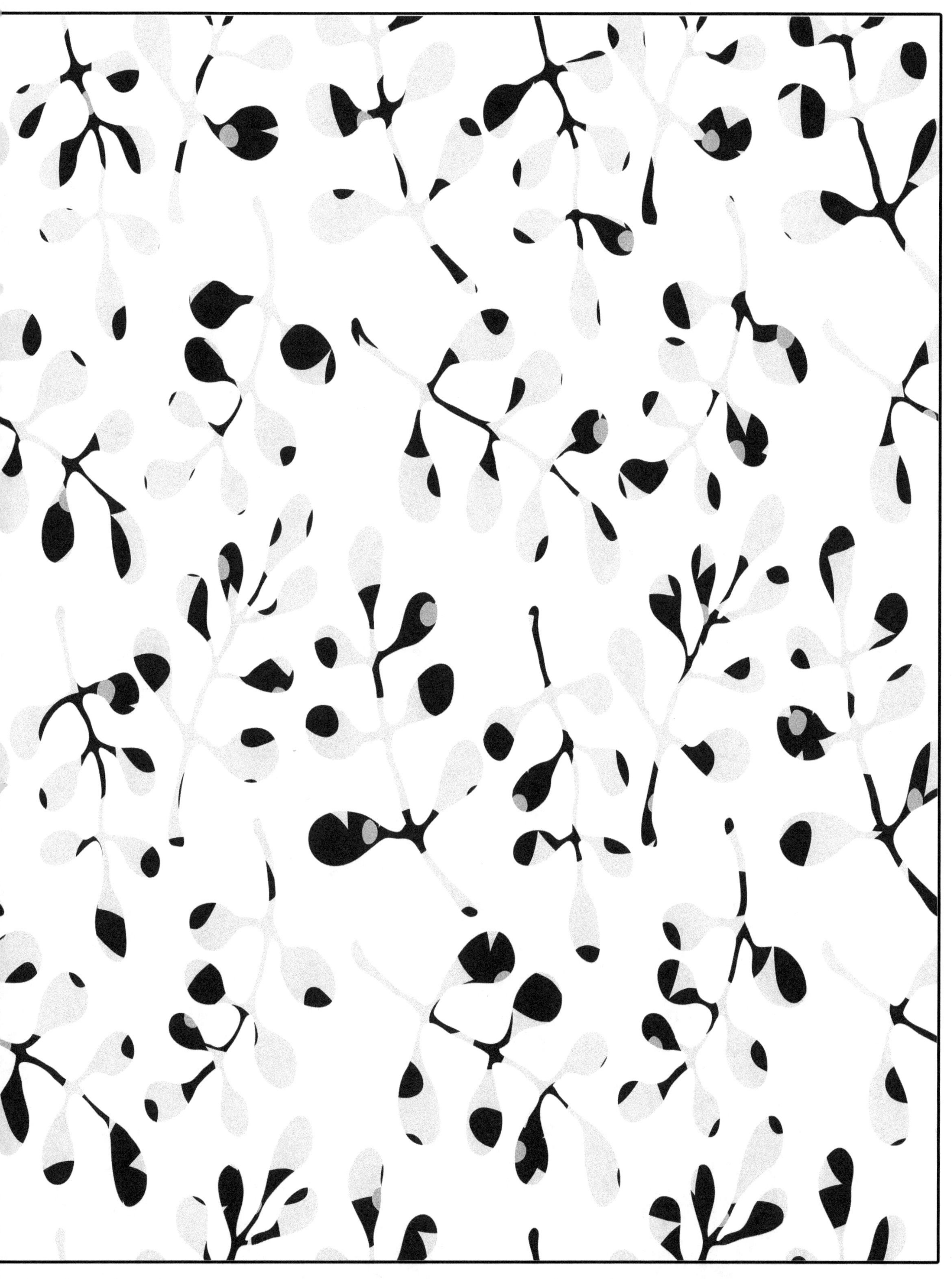

This page deliberately left blank.

As some markers can bleed through,
you may want to place a piece of paper, or wax paper,
between images.

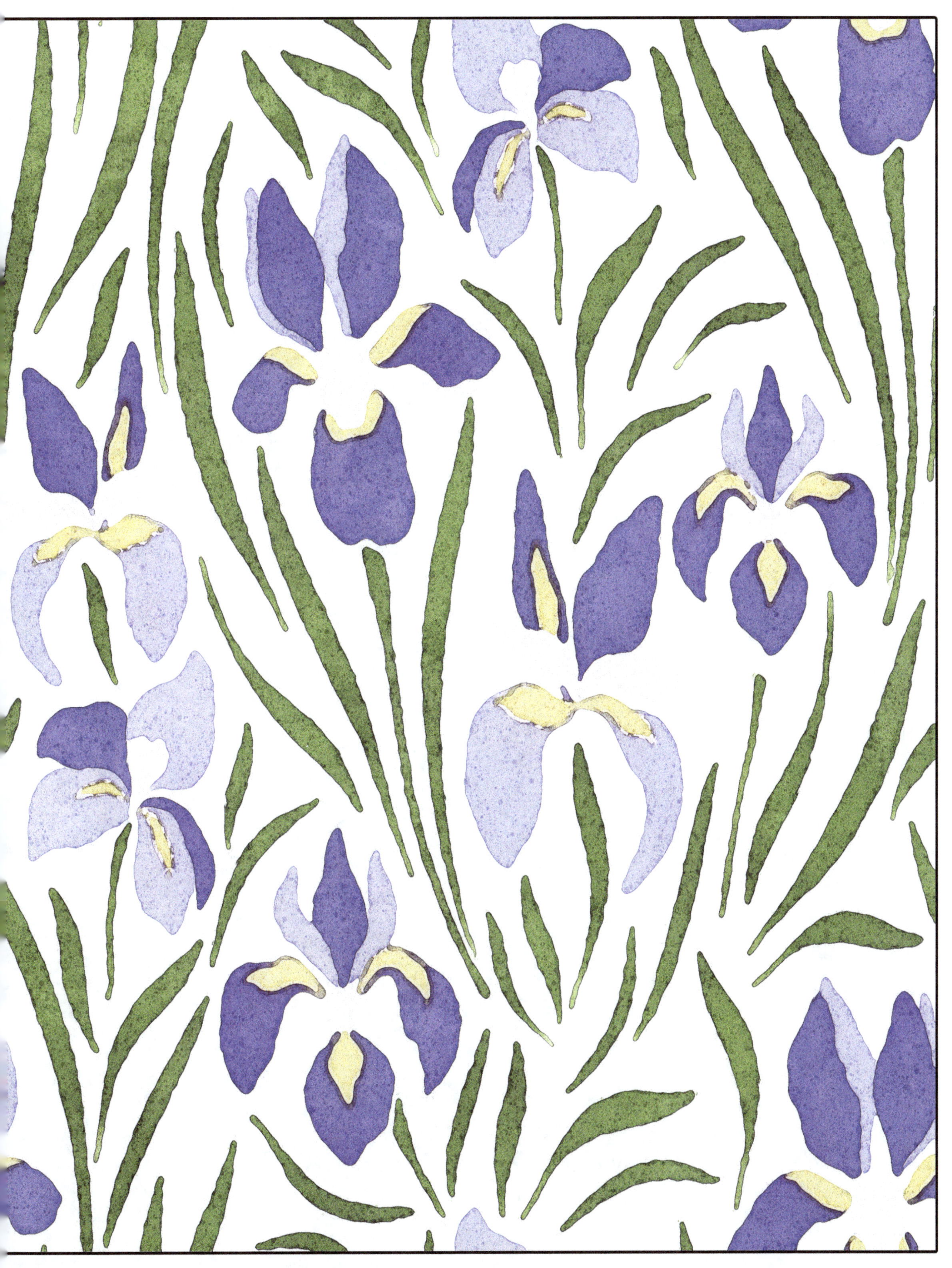

This page deliberately left blank.

As some markers can bleed through,
you may want to place a piece of paper, or wax paper,
between images.

This page deliberately left blank.

As some markers can bleed through,
you may want to place a piece of paper, or wax paper,
between images.

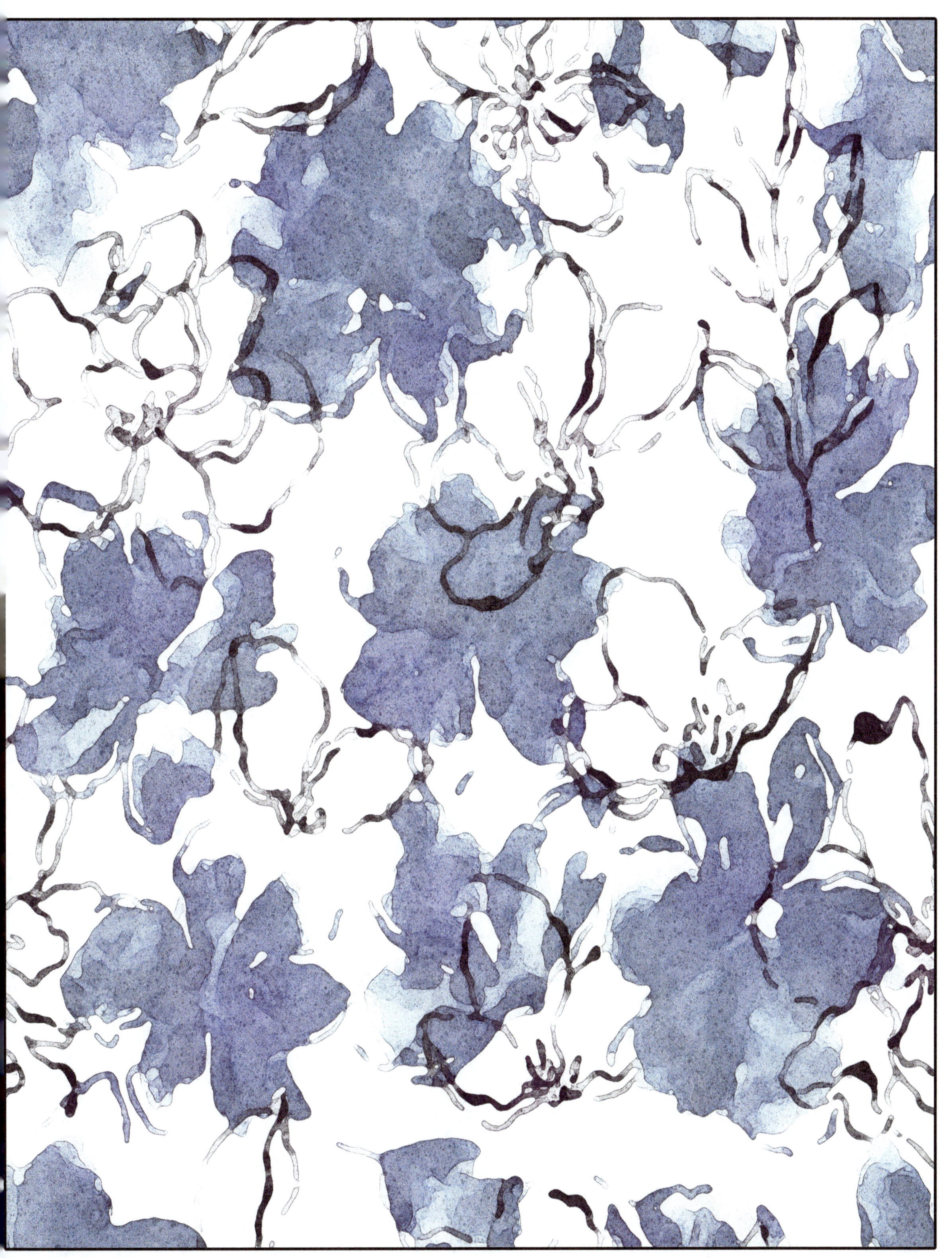

This page deliberately left blank.

As some markers can bleed through,
you may want to place a piece of paper, or wax paper,
between images.

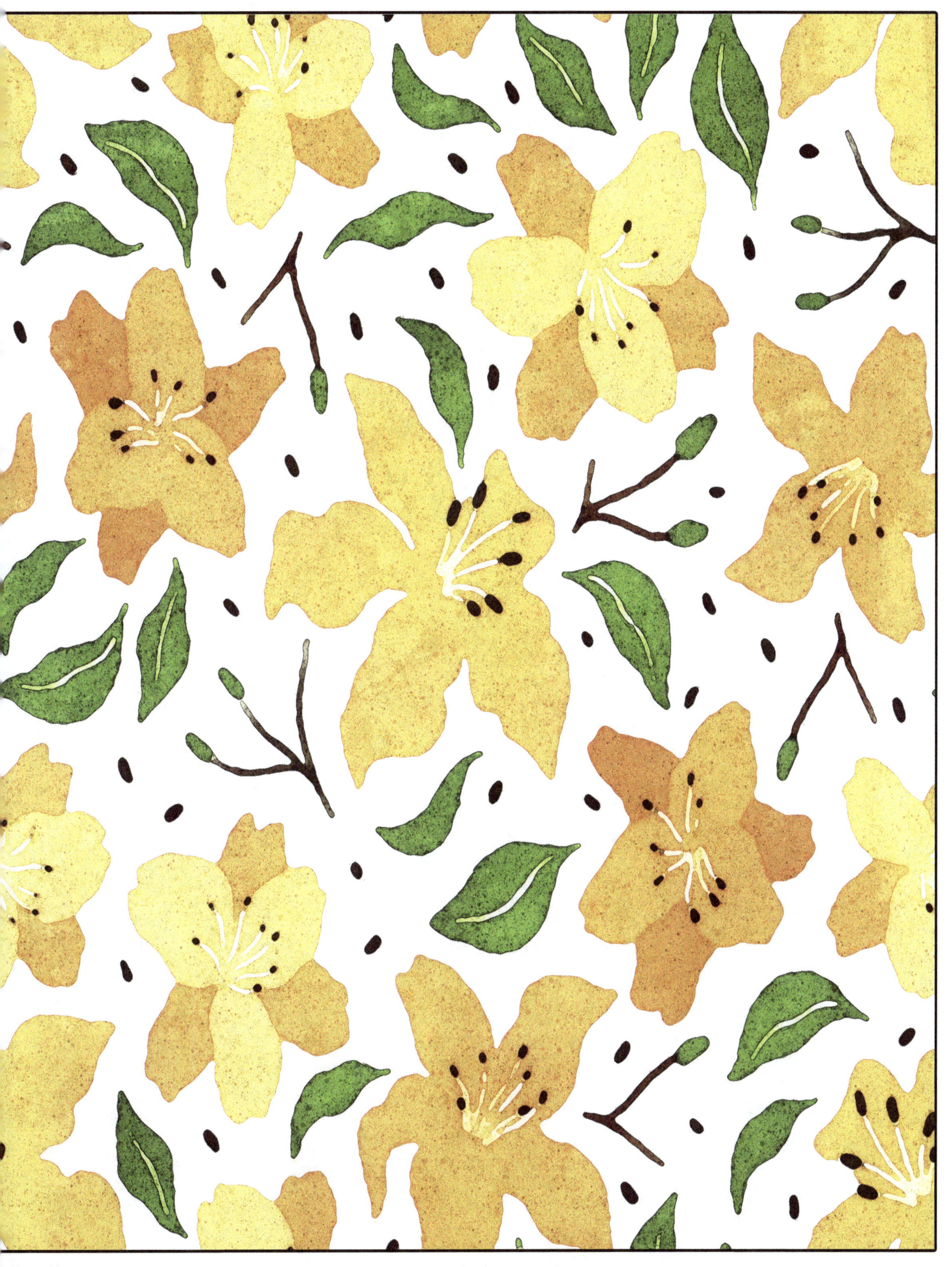

This page deliberately left blank.

As some markers can bleed through,
you may want to place a piece of paper, or wax paper,
between images.

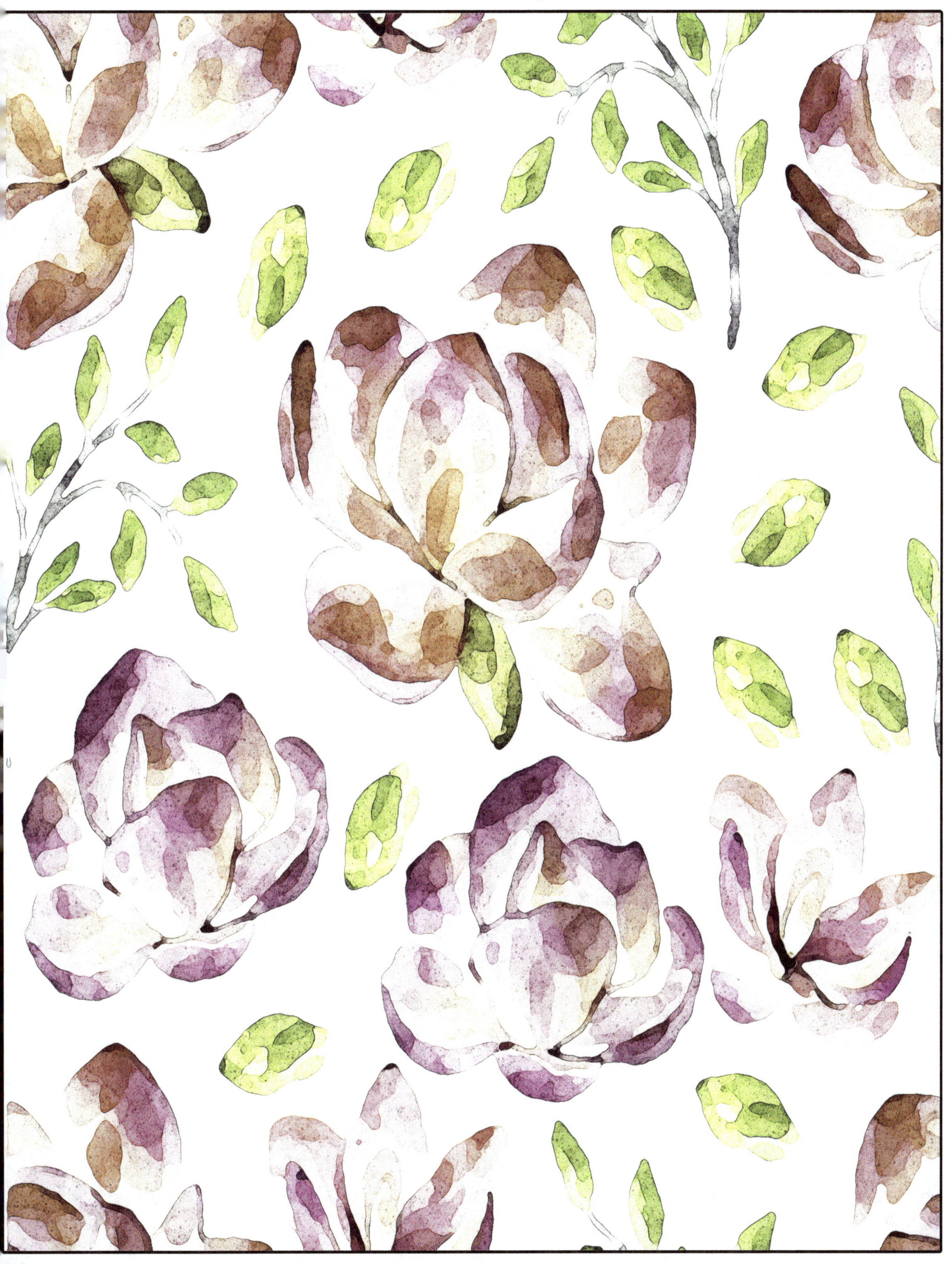

This page deliberately left blank.

As some markers can bleed through,
you may want to place a piece of paper, or wax paper,
between images.

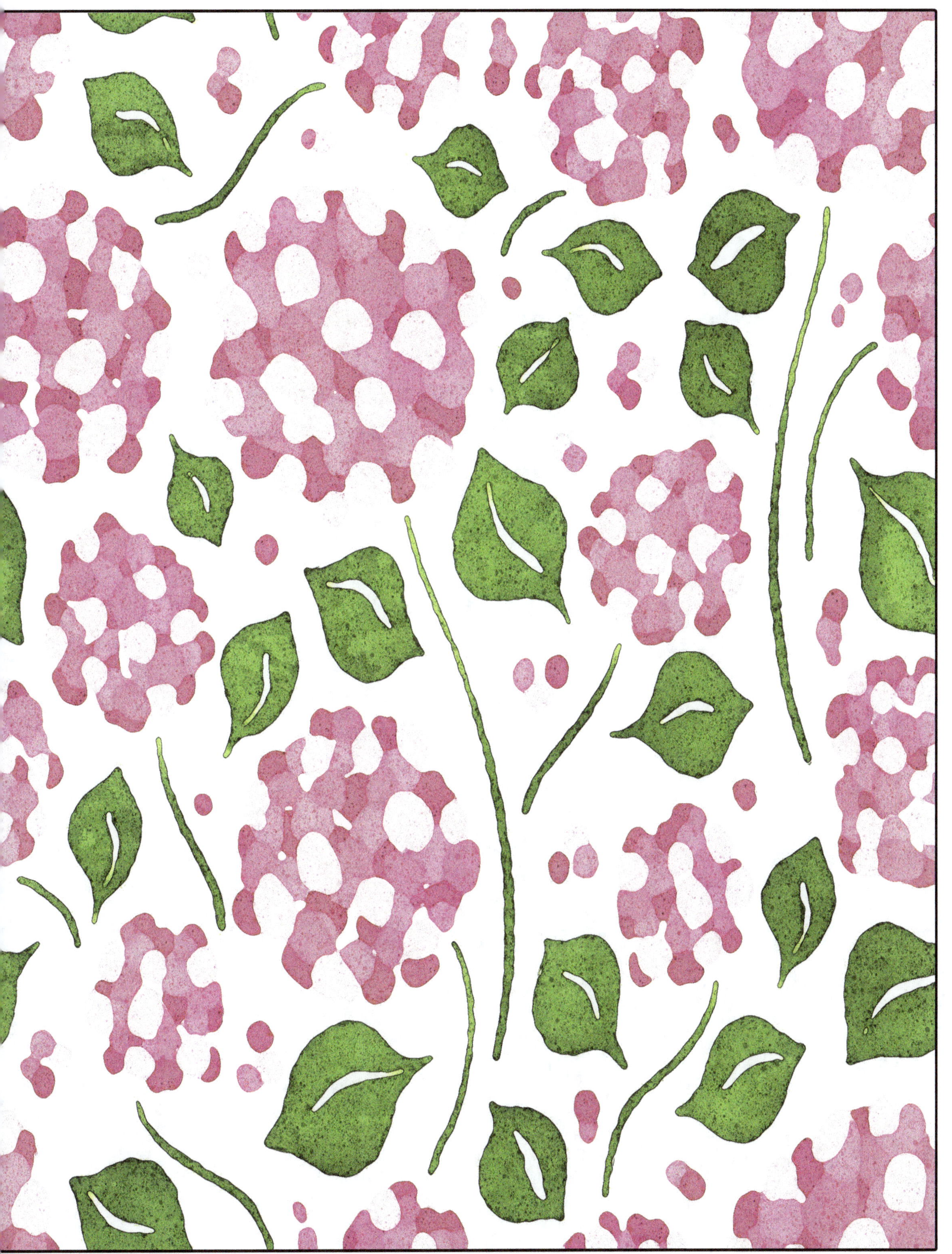

This page deliberately left blank.

As some markers can bleed through,
you may want to place a piece of paper, or wax paper,
between images.

This page deliberately left blank.

As some markers can bleed through, you may want to place a piece of paper, or wax paper, between images.

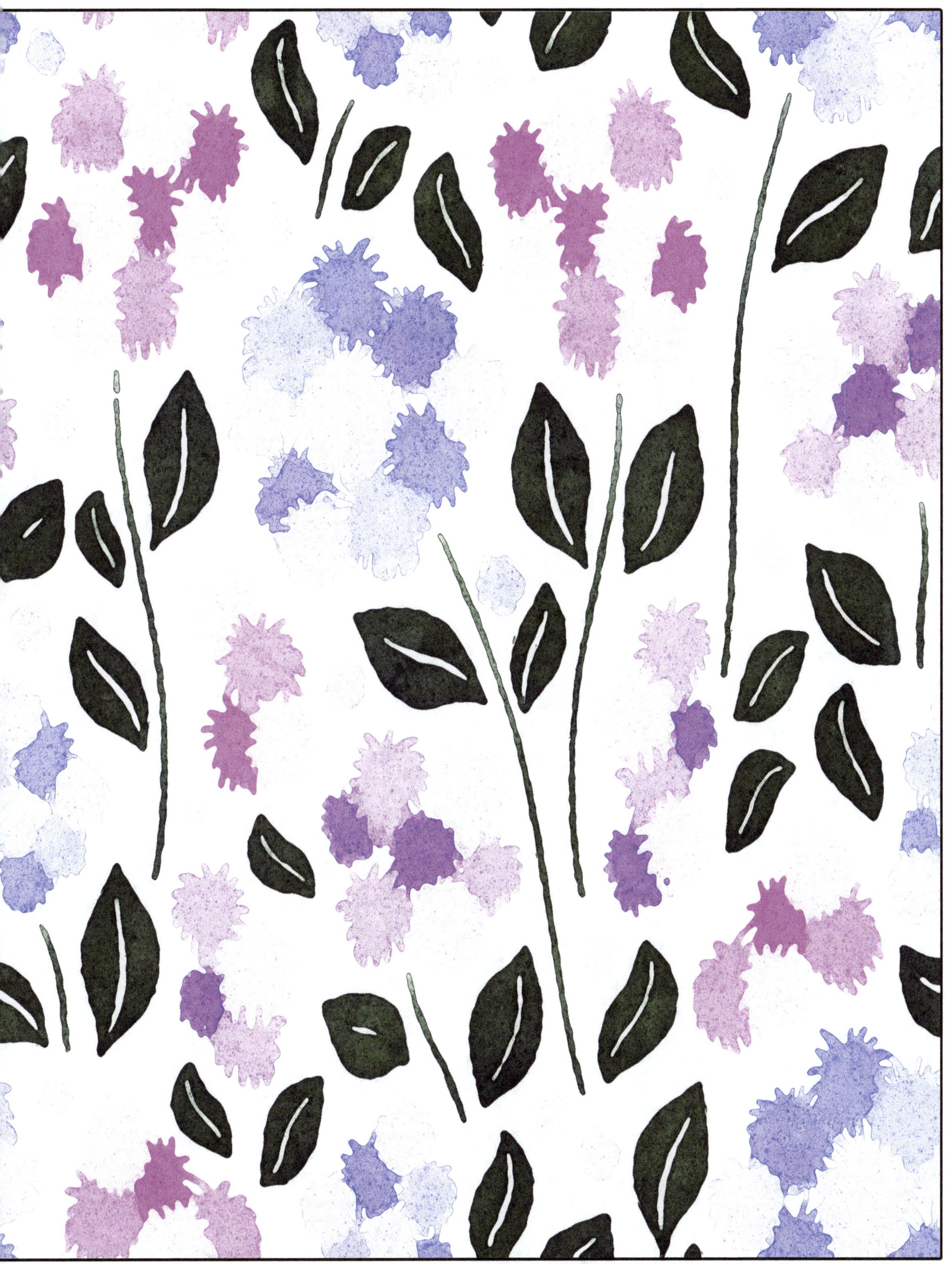

This page deliberately left blank.

As some markers can bleed through,
you may want to place a piece of paper, or wax paper,
between images.

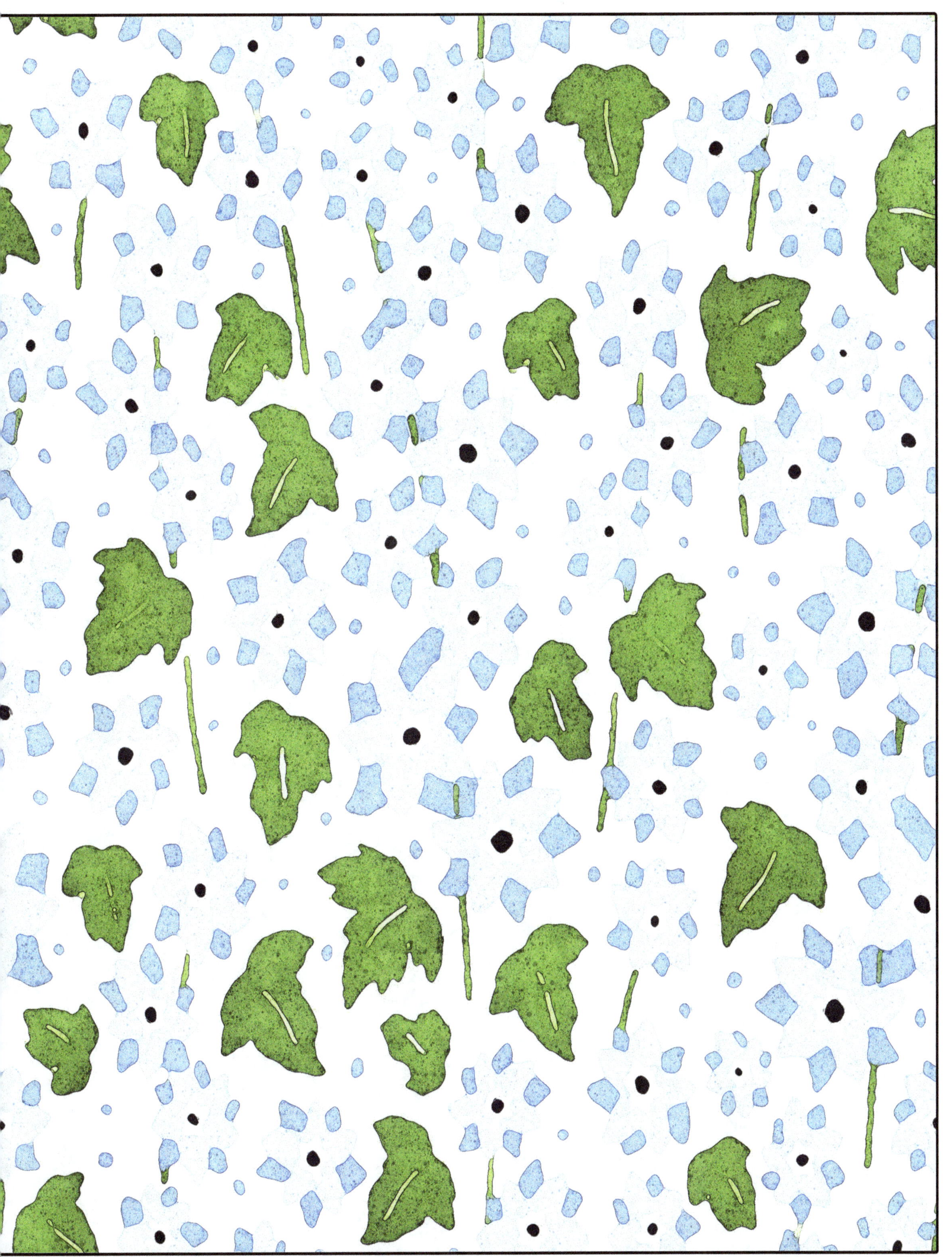

This page deliberately left blank.

As some markers can bleed through,
you may want to place a piece of paper, or wax paper,
between images.

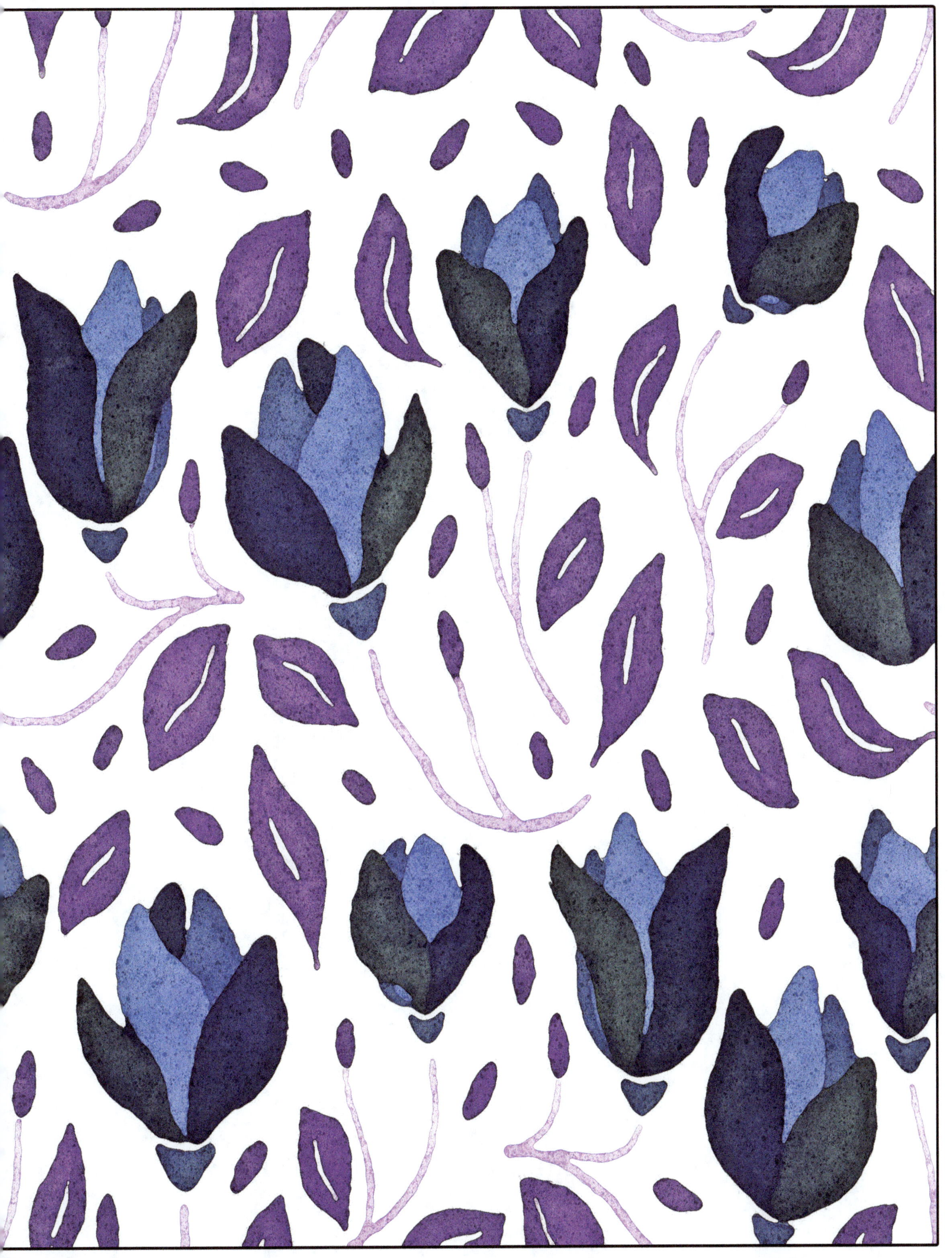

This page deliberately left blank.

As some markers can bleed through,
you may want to place a piece of paper, or wax paper,
between images.

This page deliberately left blank.

As some markers can bleed through,
you may want to place a piece of paper, or wax paper,
between images.

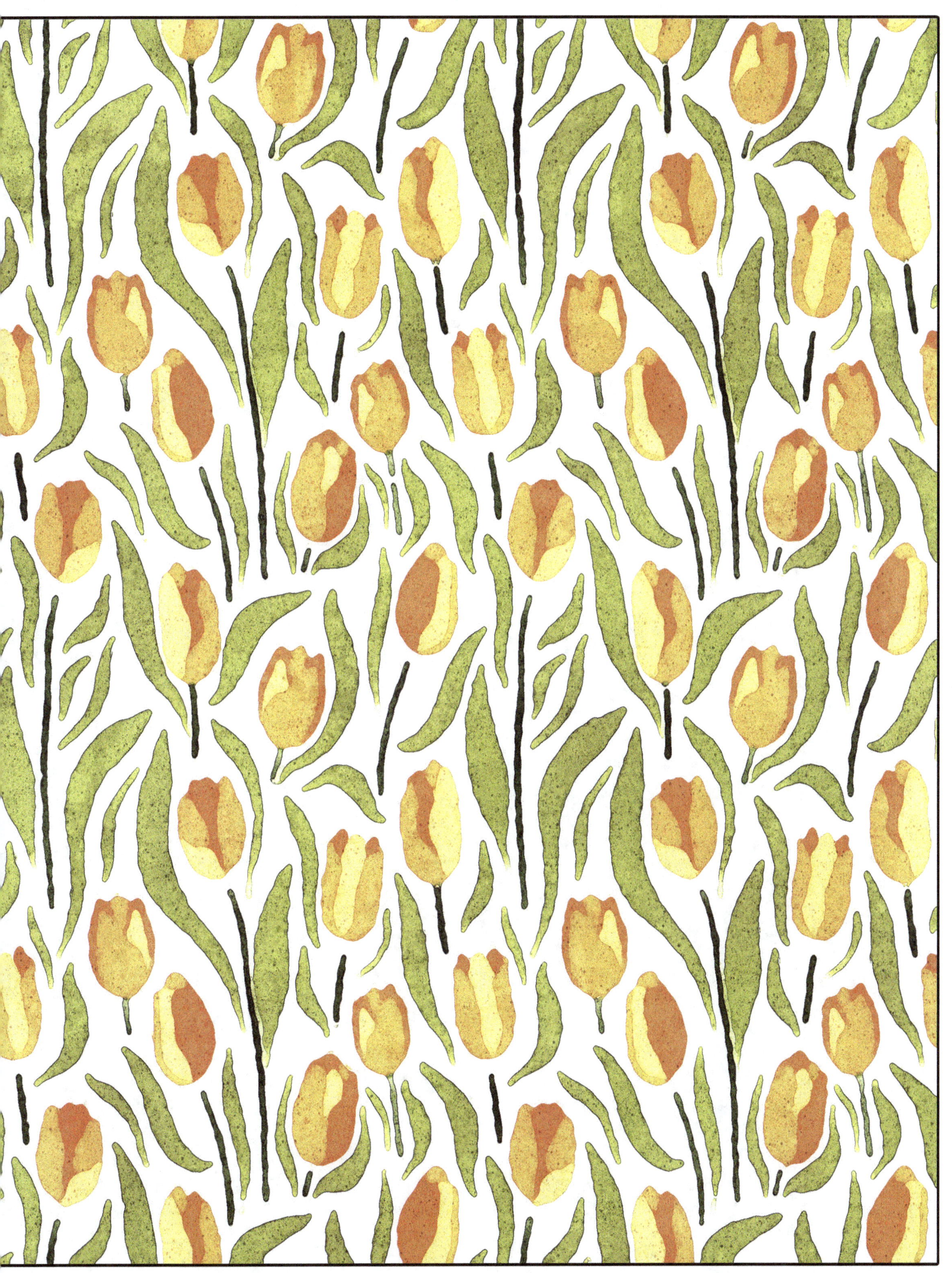

This page deliberately left blank.

As some markers can bleed through,
you may want to place a piece of paper, or wax paper,
between images.

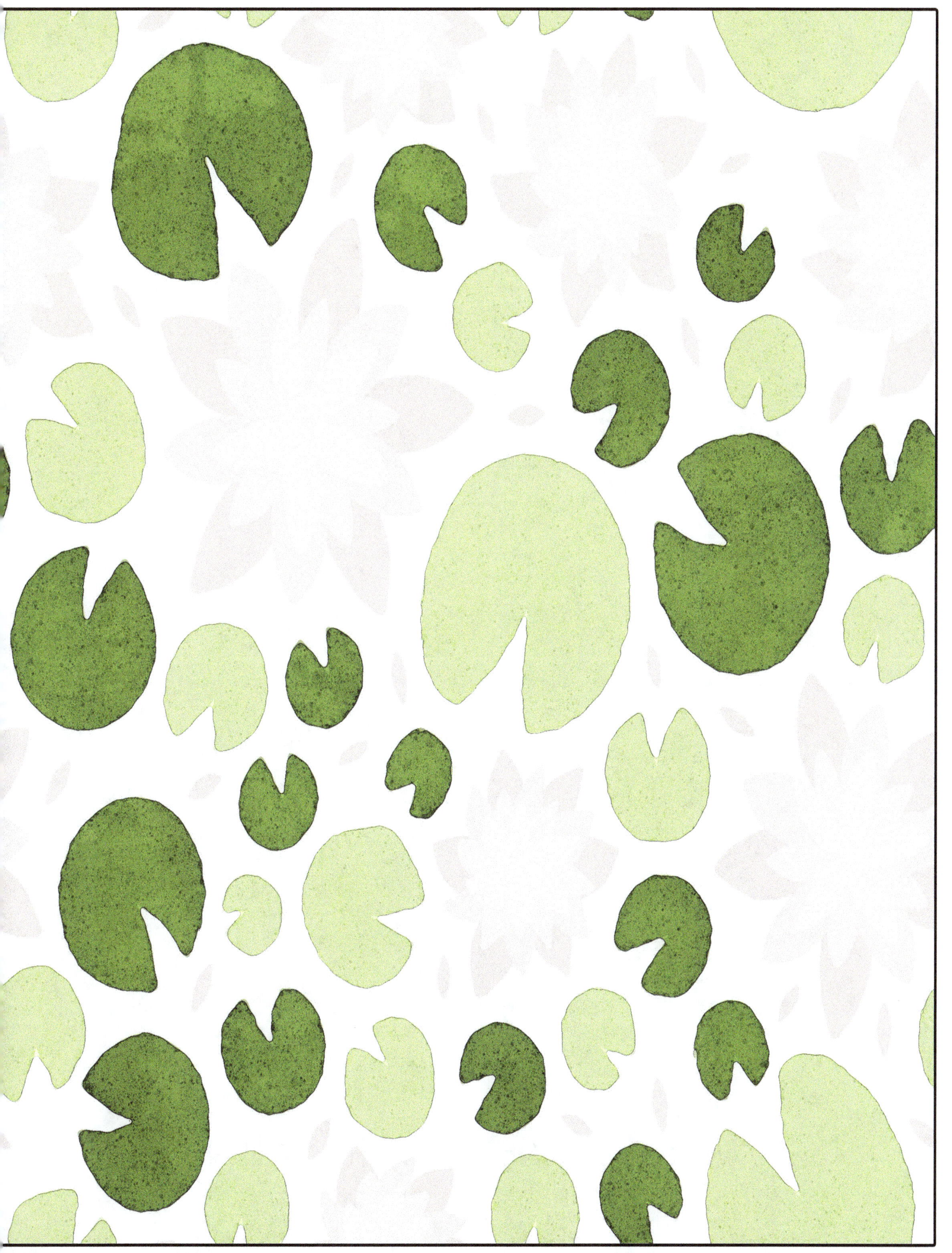

This page deliberately left blank.

As some markers can bleed through,
you may want to place a piece of paper, or wax paper,
between images.

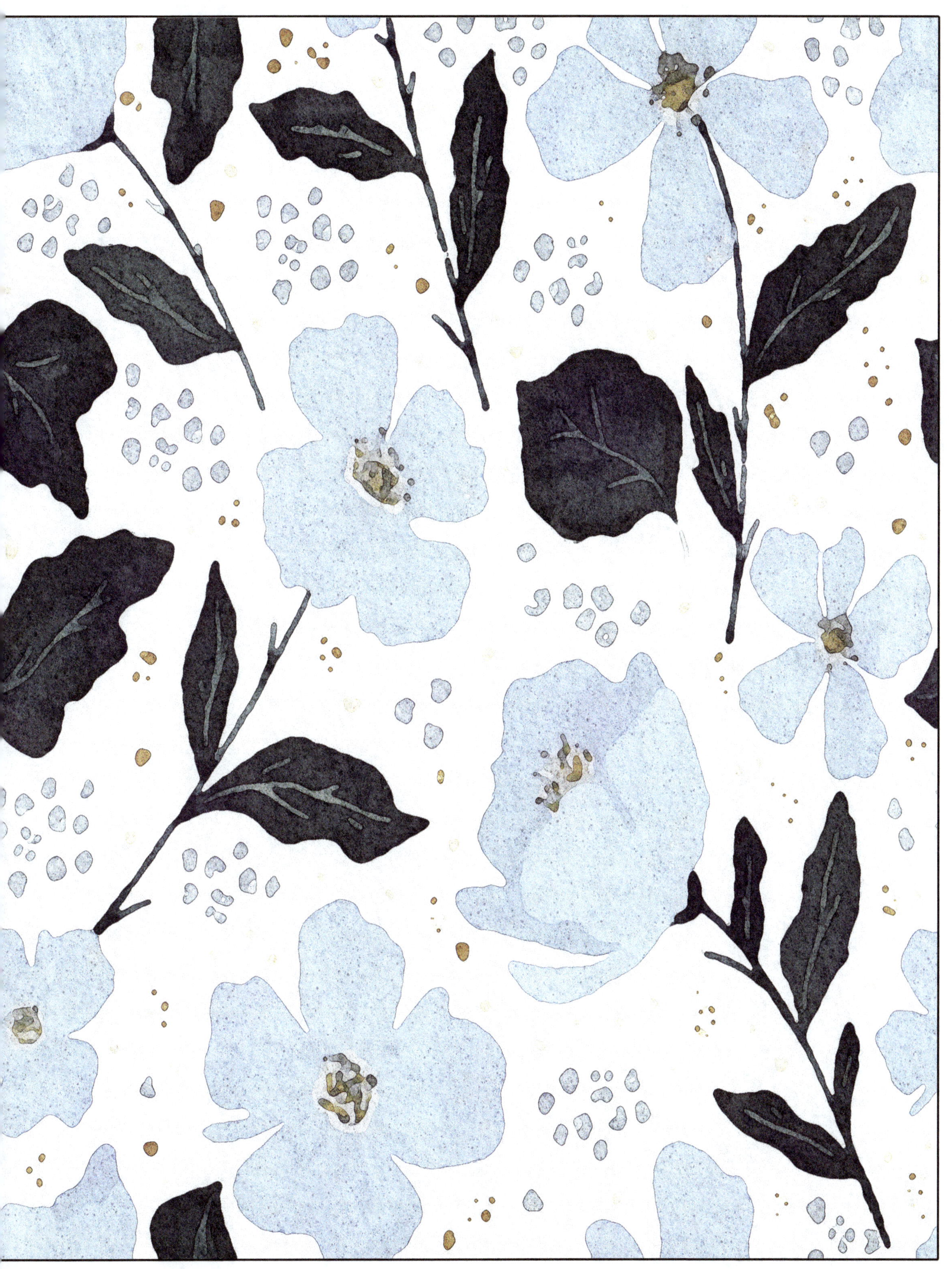

This page deliberately left blank.

As some markers can bleed through,
you may want to place a piece of paper, or wax paper,
between images.

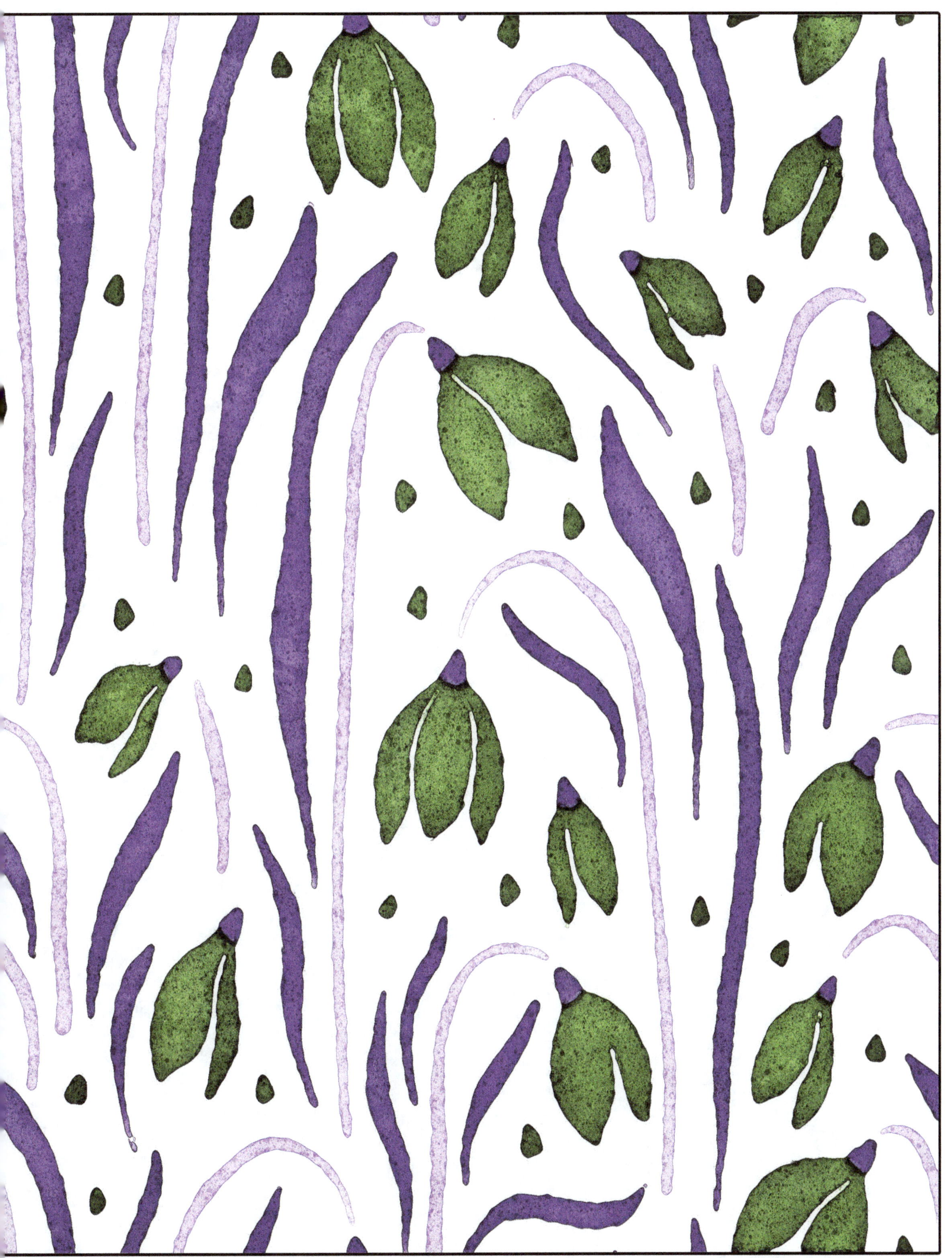

This page deliberately left blank.

As some markers can bleed through,
you may want to place a piece of paper, or wax paper,
between images.

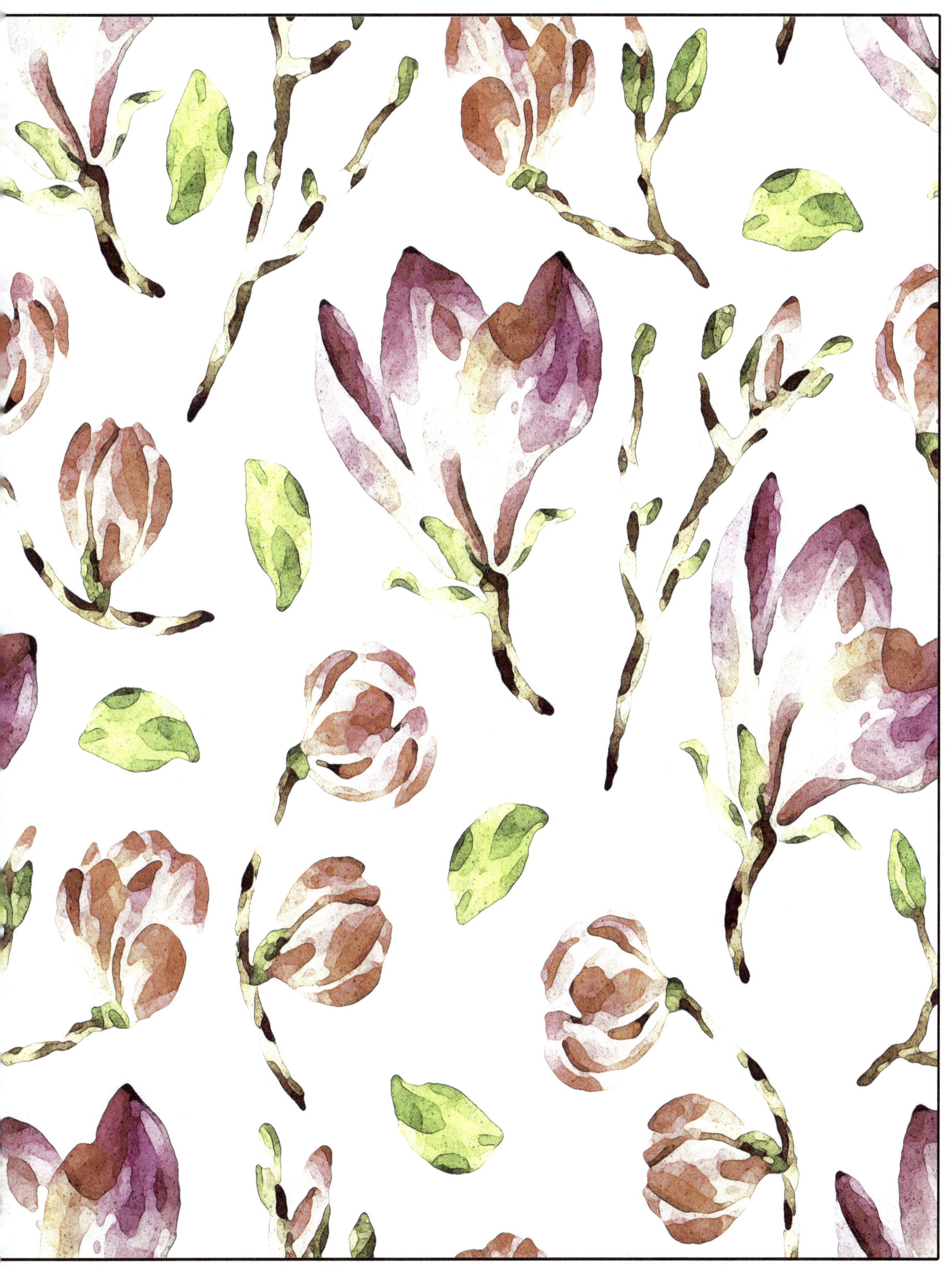

This page deliberately left blank.

As some markers can bleed through,
you may want to place a piece of paper, or wax paper,
between images.

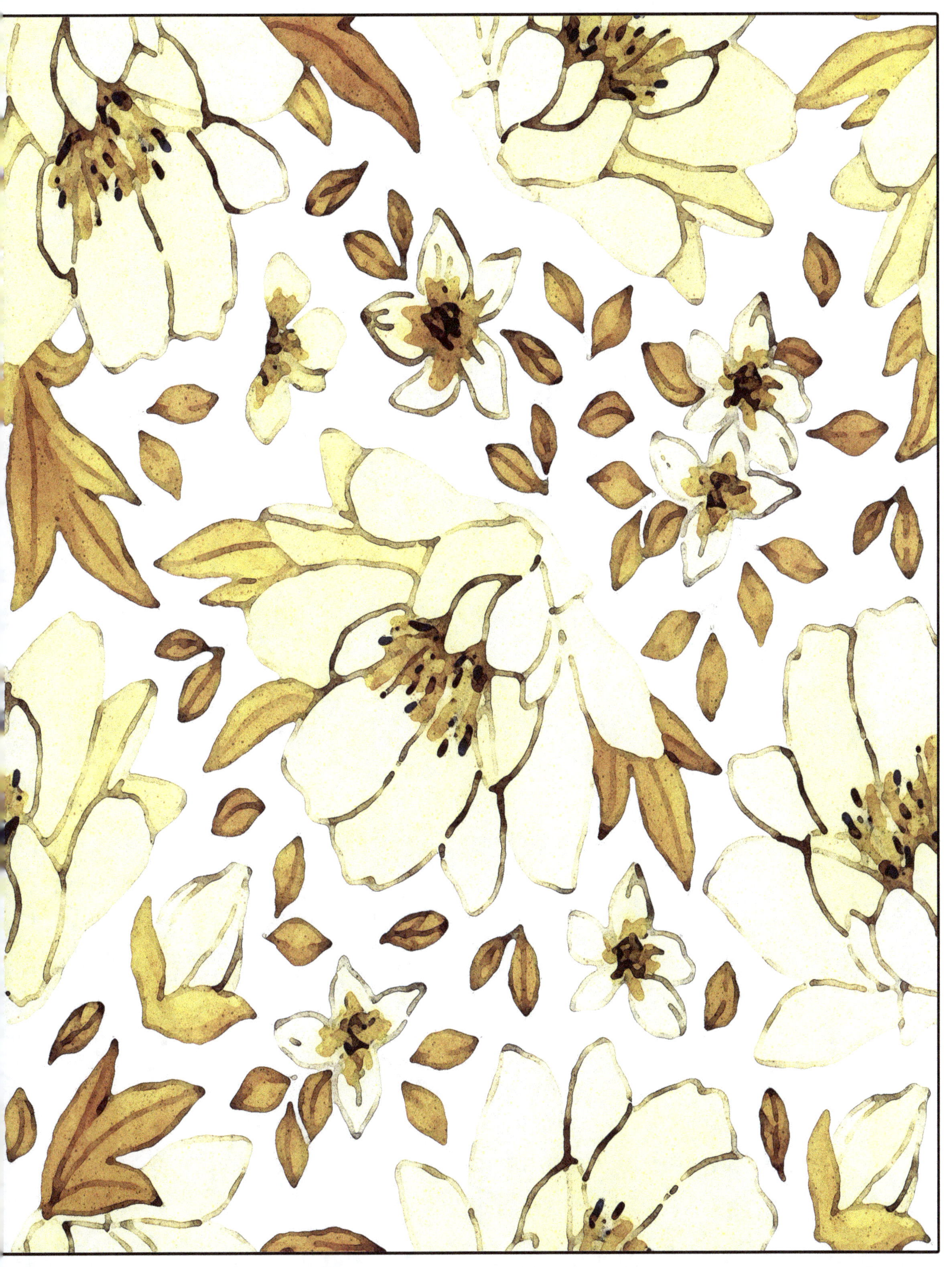

This page deliberately left blank.

As some markers can bleed through,
you may want to place a piece of paper, or wax paper,
between images.

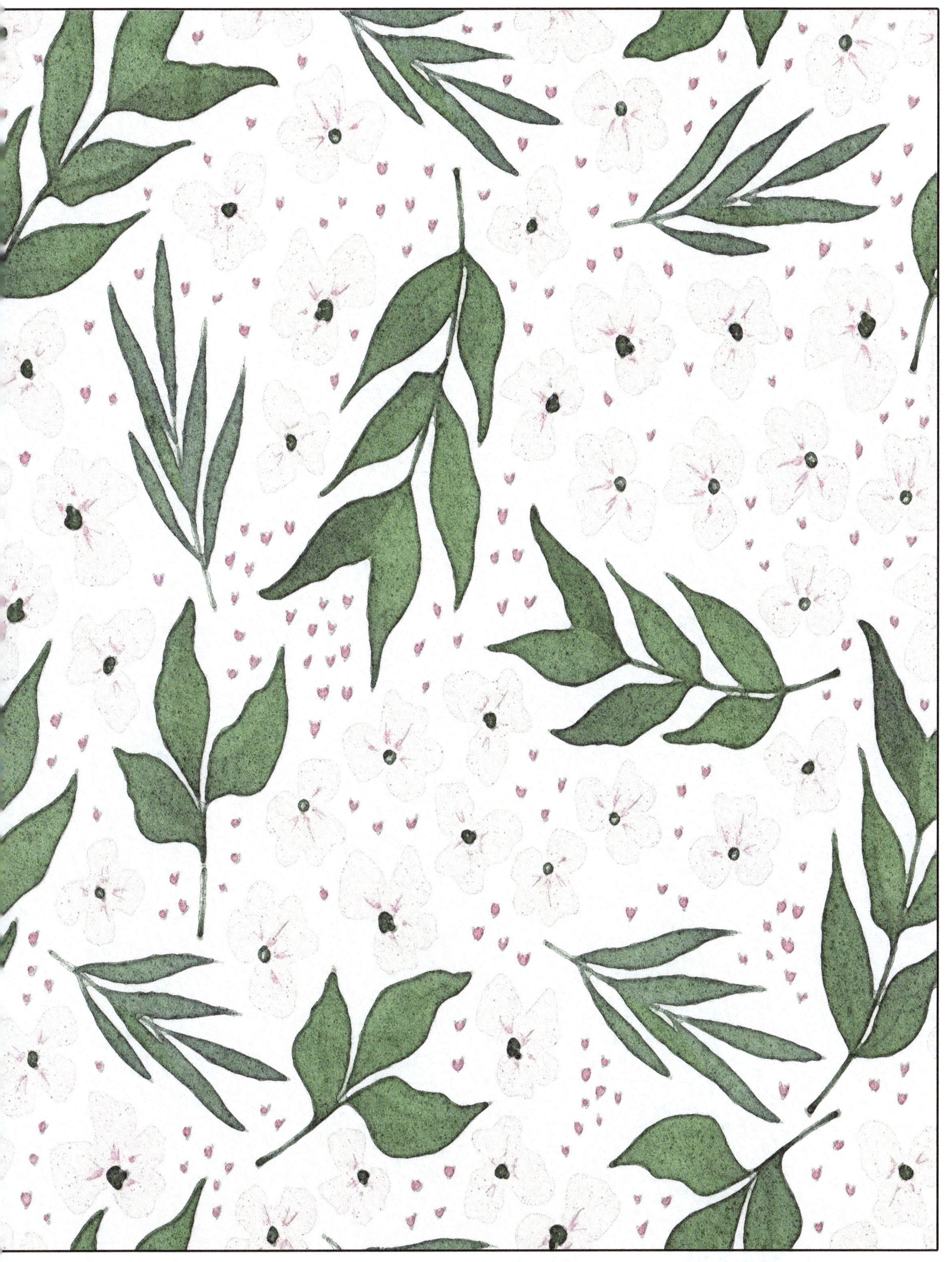

This page deliberately left blank.

As some markers can bleed through,
you may want to place a piece of paper, or wax paper,
between images.

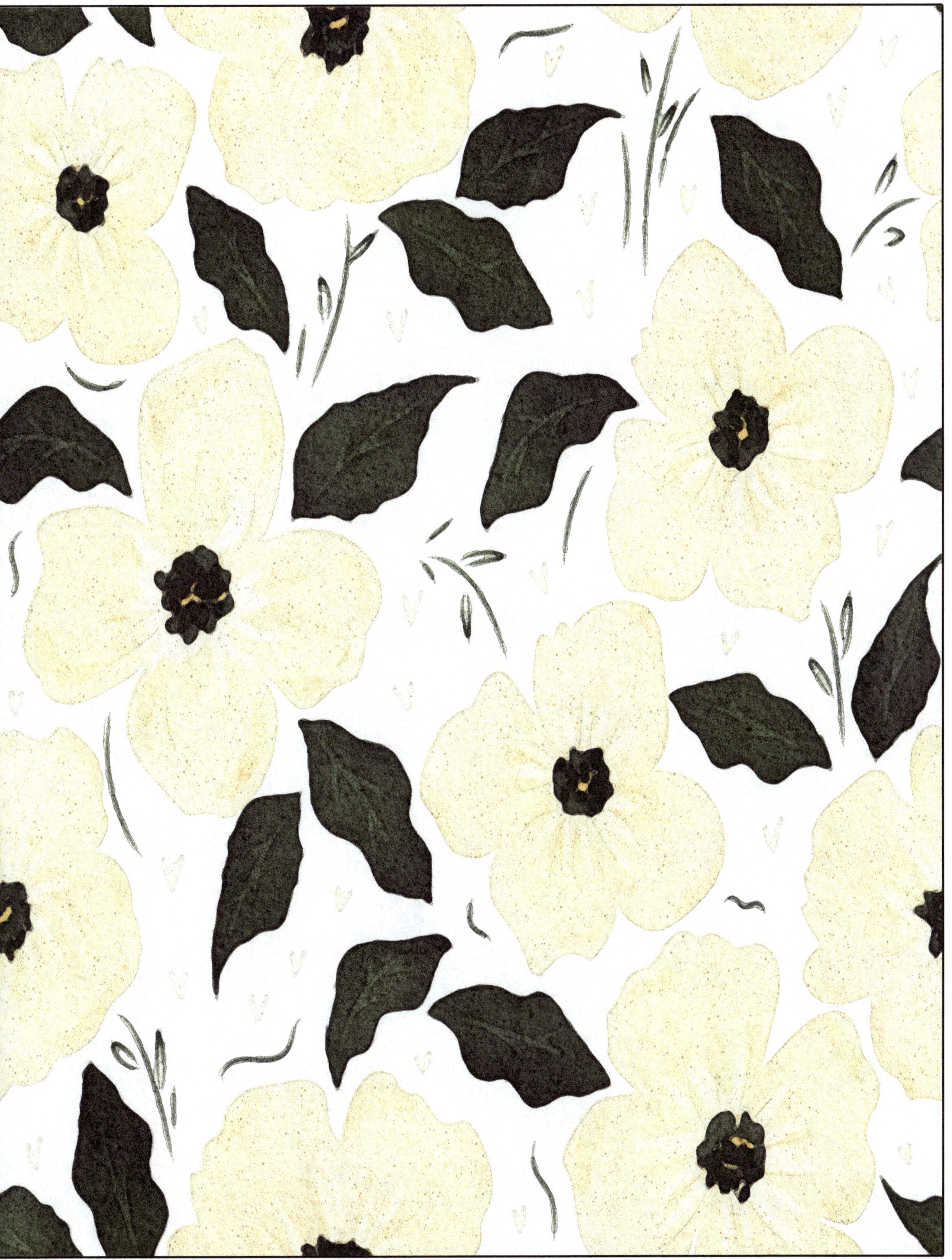

This page deliberately left blank.

As some markers can bleed through,
you may want to place a piece of paper, or wax paper,
between images.

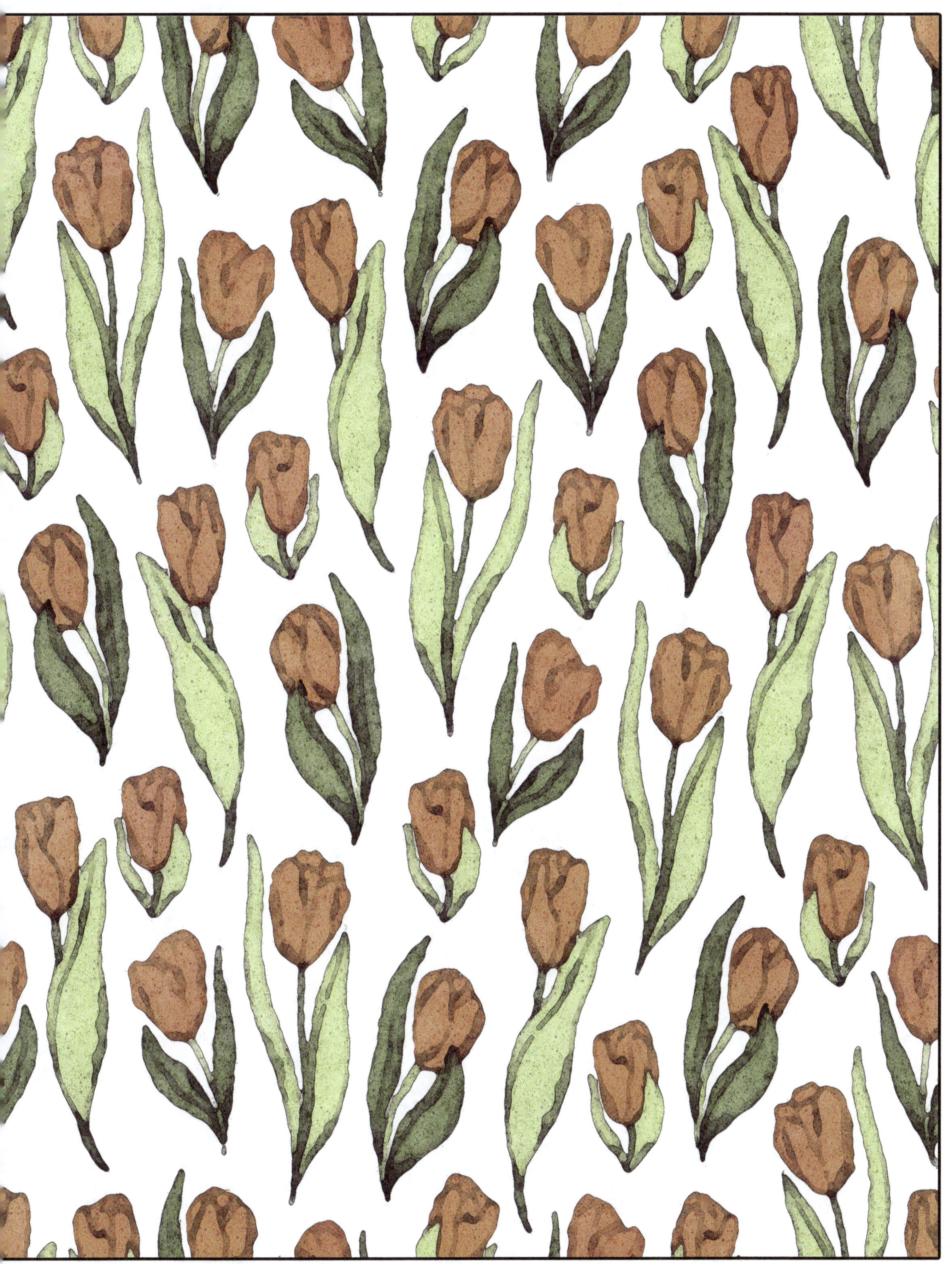

This page deliberately left blank.

As some markers can bleed through,
you may want to place a piece of paper, or wax paper,
between images.

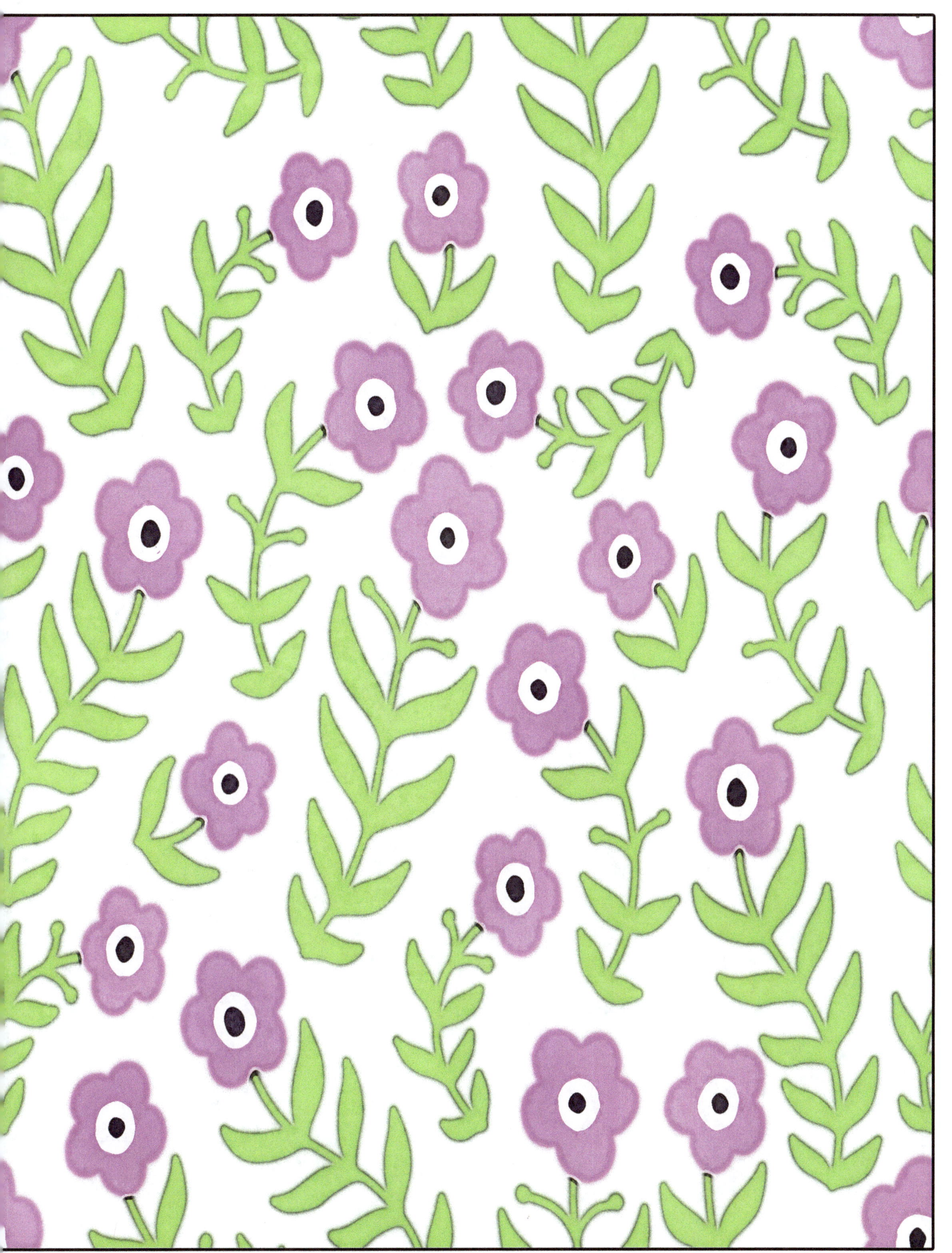

This page deliberately left blank.

As some markers can bleed through,
you may want to place a piece of paper, or wax paper,
between images.

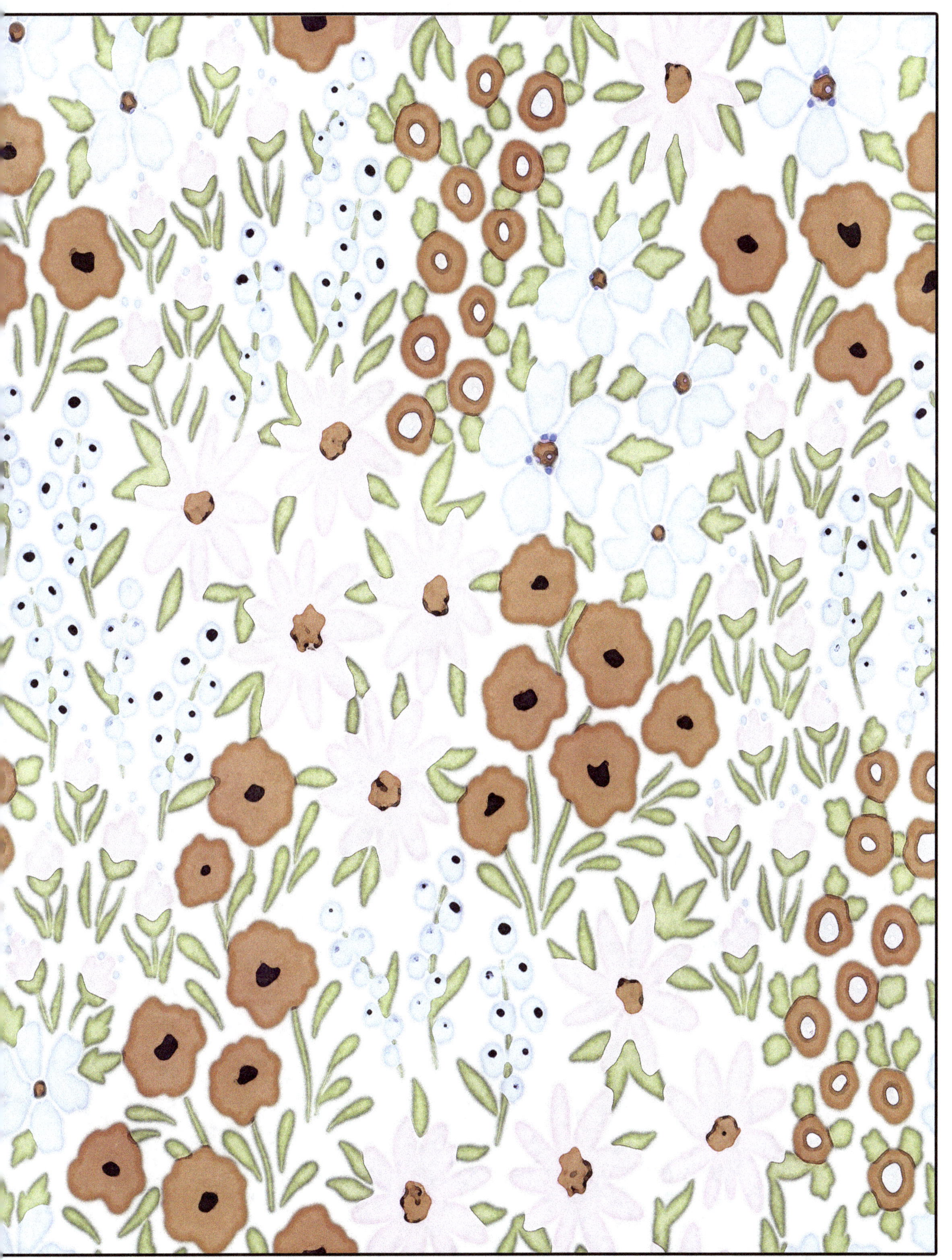

This page deliberately left blank.

As some markers can bleed through,
you may want to place a piece of paper, or wax paper,
between images.

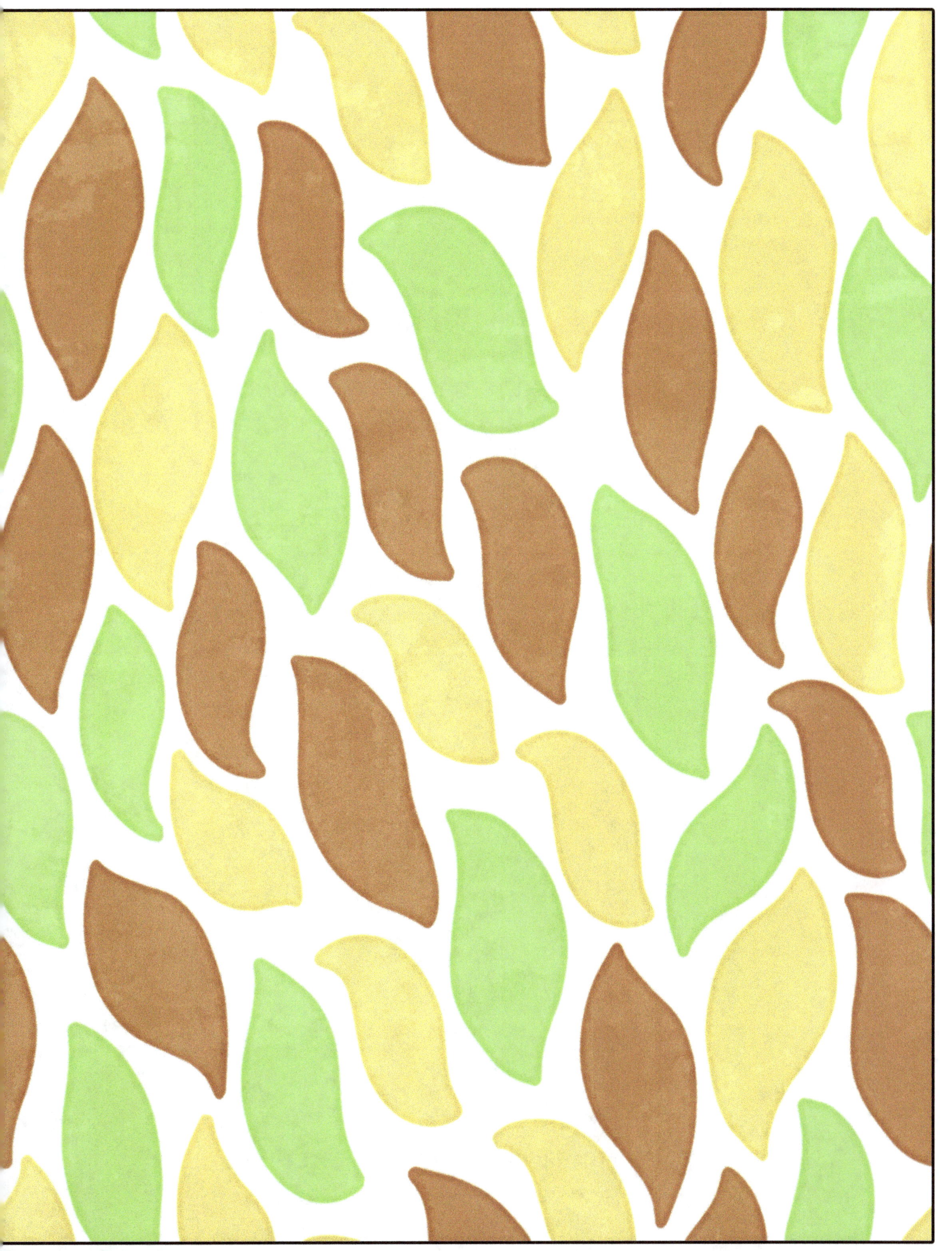

This page deliberately left blank.

As some markers can bleed through,
you may want to place a piece of paper, or wax paper,
between images.

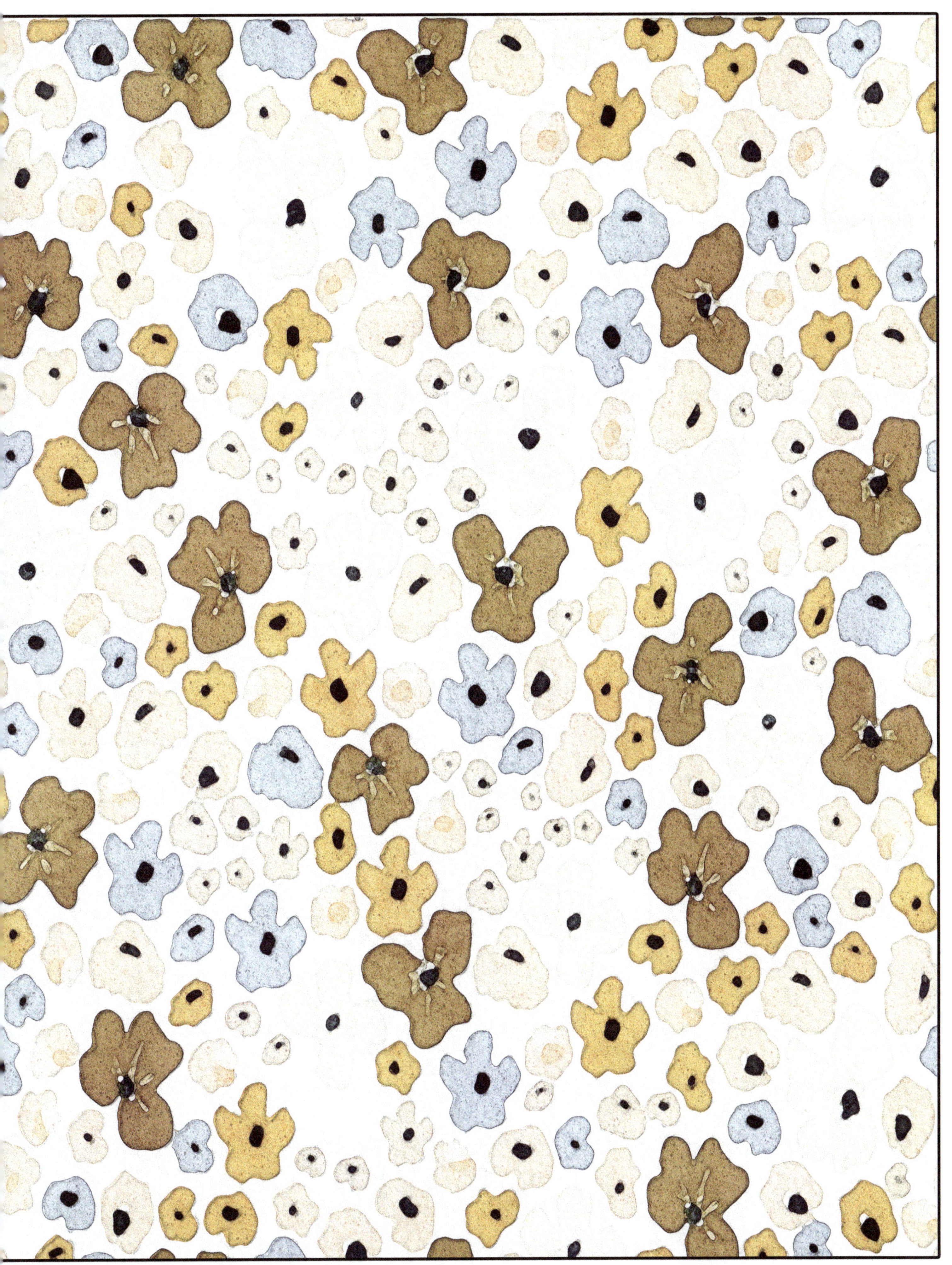

This page deliberately left blank.

As some markers can bleed through,
you may want to place a piece of paper, or wax paper,
between images.

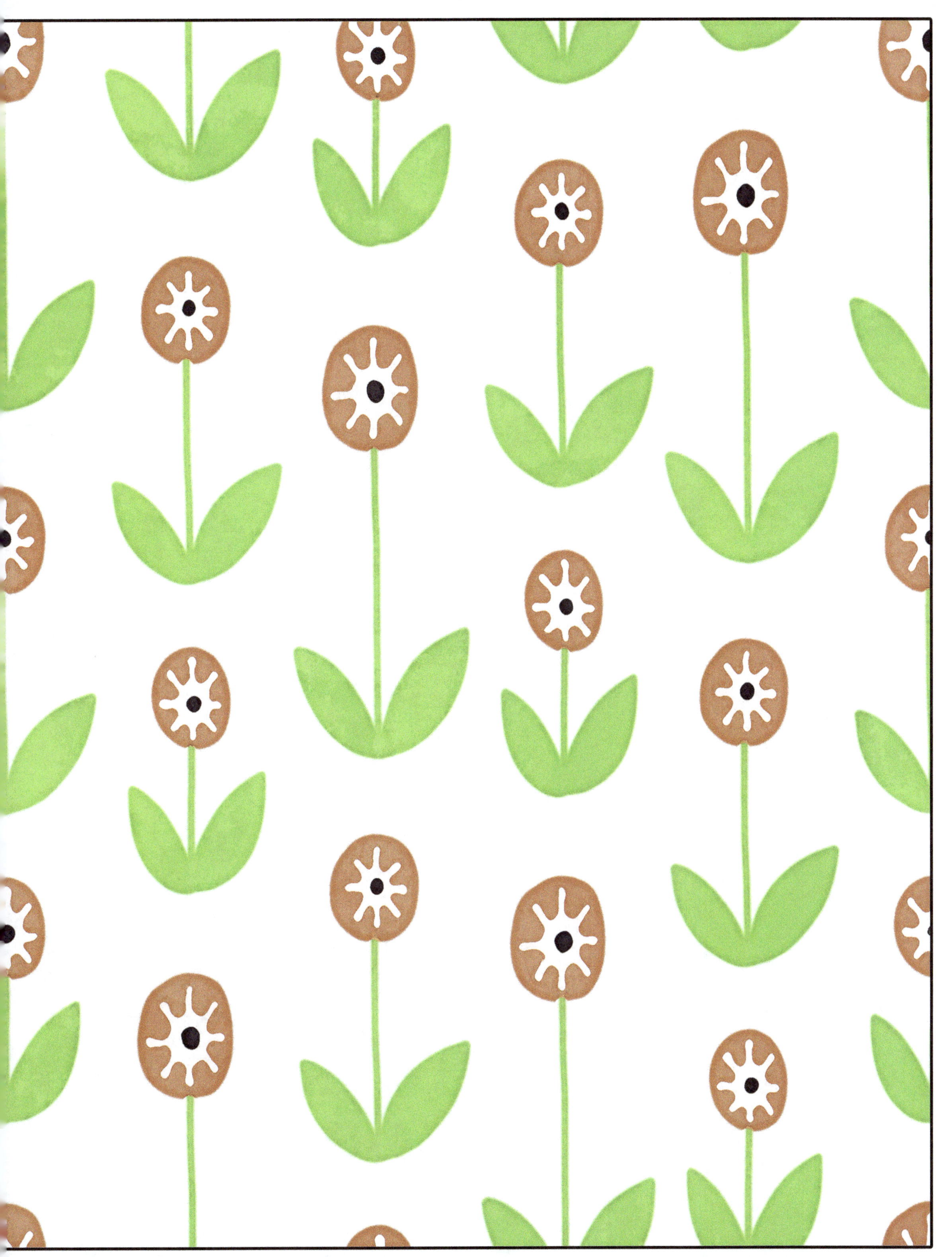

This page deliberately left blank.

As some markers can bleed through,
you may want to place a piece of paper, or wax paper,
between images.

If you enjoyed this book, please consider leaving a review on Amazon to help others find it.

To find more activity books & journals from Kat Mariaca, please visit my author page on Amazon.

Thank you.

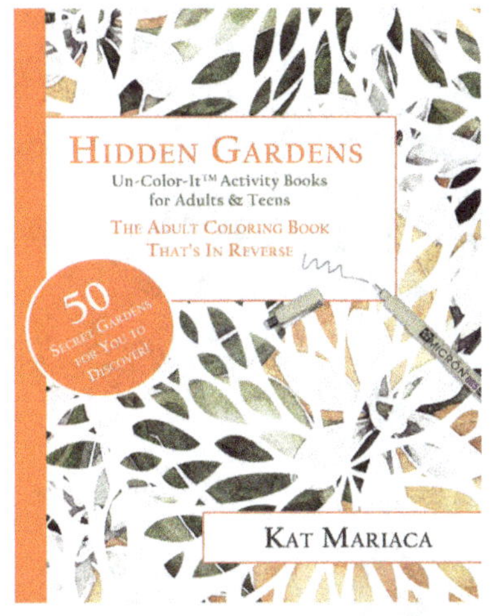


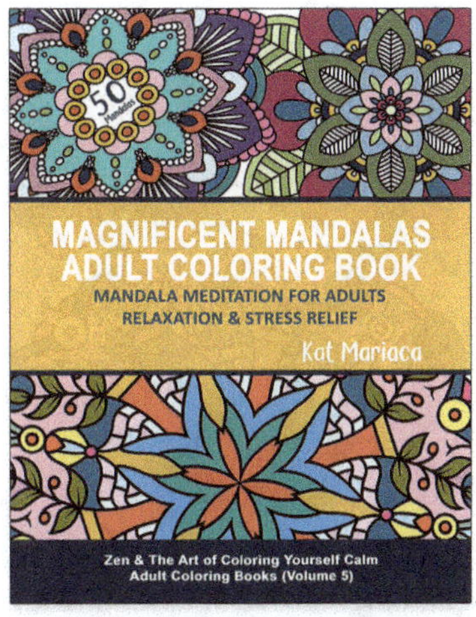


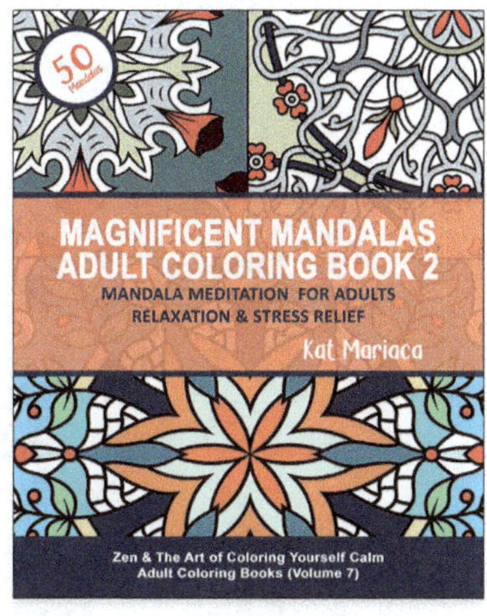


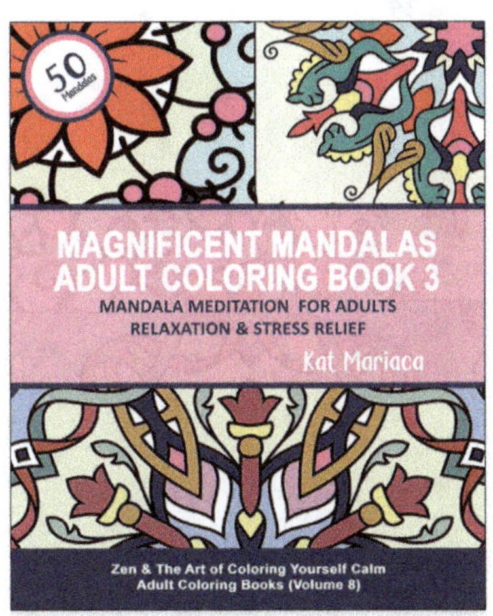


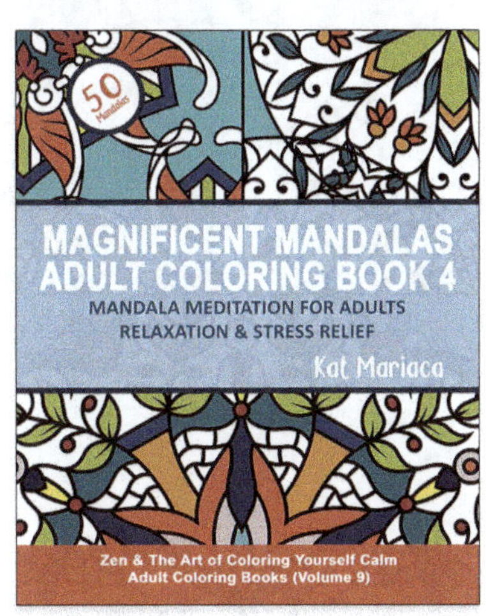


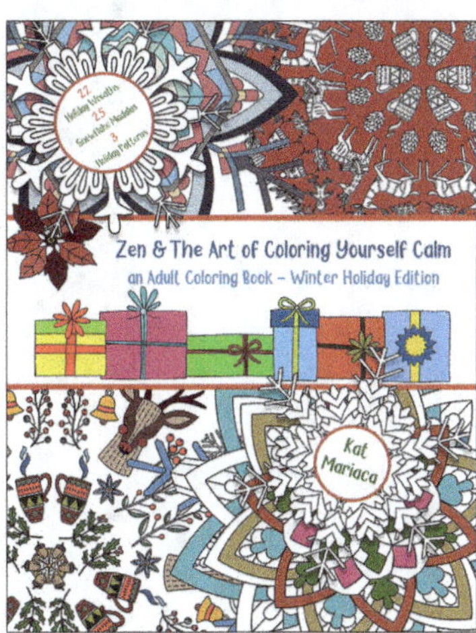


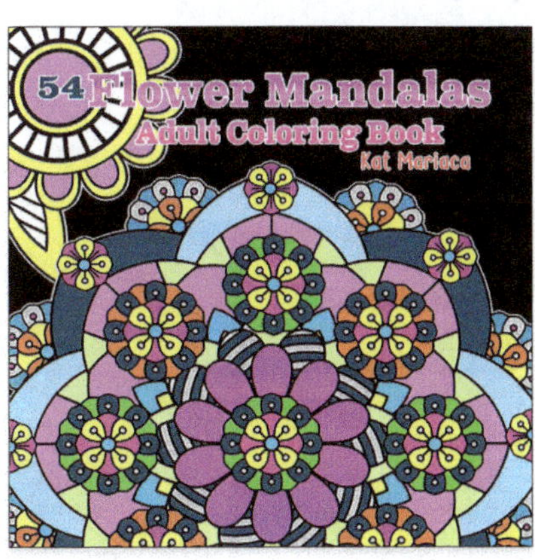


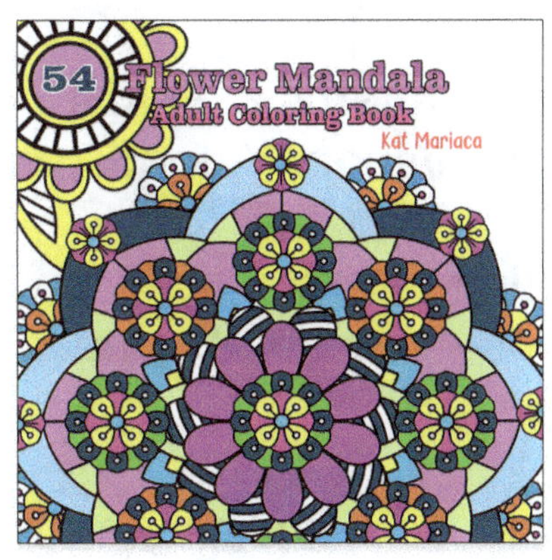


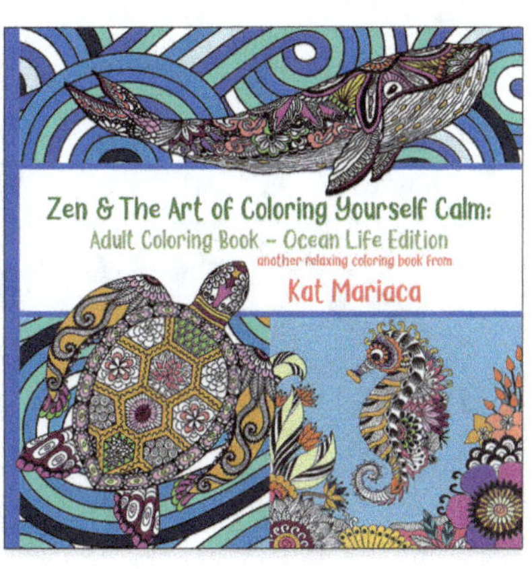

## More books by Kat Mariaca for you to enjoy:

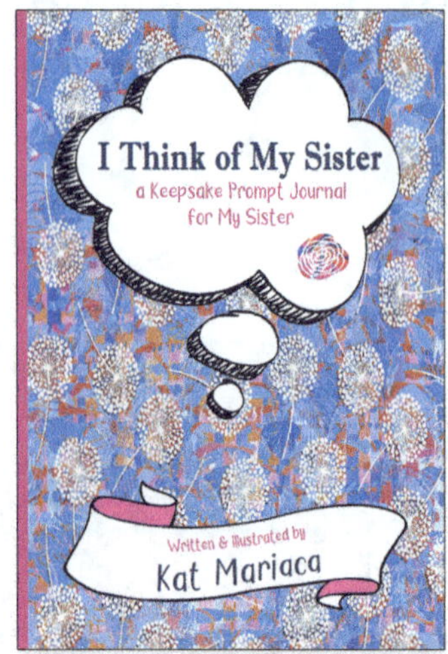


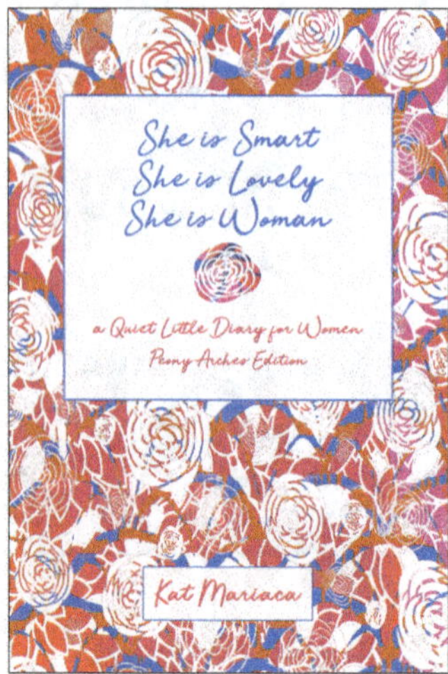


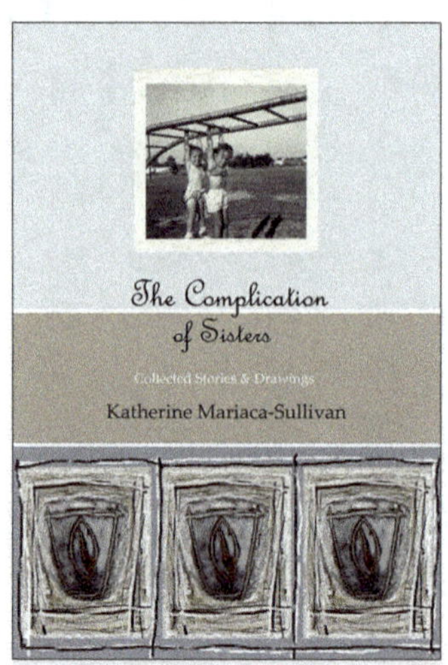


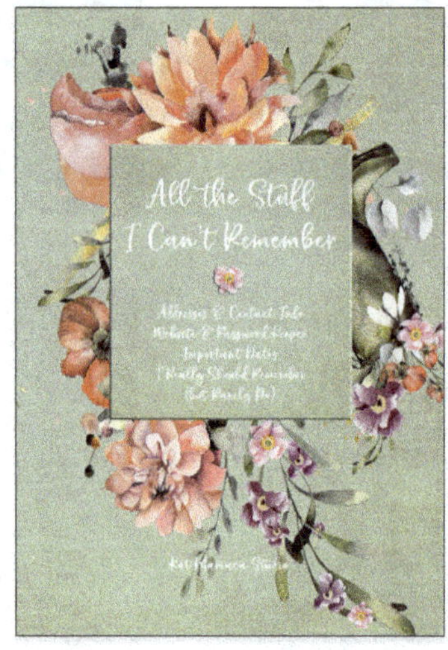


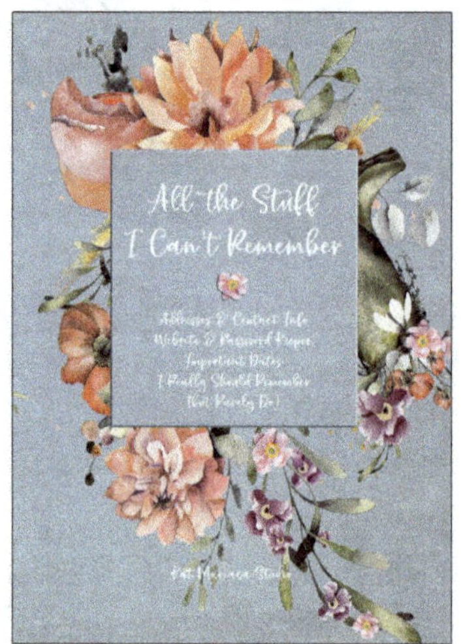


Art prints:
Etsy.com/shops/AdornYourWallsArt

Patterns & PNGs
Etsy.com/shops/AdornCreatives

Greeting Cards, Gifts & Journals
Etsy.com/Shops/KatMariacaStudio

Art Prints:
Madaket Lane on Amazon

www.ingramcontent.com/pod-product-compliance
Lightning Source LLC
LaVergne TN
LVHW080335110826
845155LV00027B/243

* 9 7 8 1 9 4 0 8 9 2 3 9 9 *